WHAT IS IT ABOUT VIRGINIA?

WHAT IS IT ABOUT VIRGINIA?

by GUY FRIDDELL

Book Layout and Jacket Design by Carl E. Larsen

Photographs from the Virginia State Chamber of Commerce and The Commonwealth Magazine

THE DIETZ PRESS, INC.
RICHMOND, VIRGINIA

To Virginia
And All Virginians
Especially
My Virginia

In 1814, to a publisher interested in having him revise *Notes on the State of Virginia,* Thomas Jefferson wrote: "The work itself indeed is nothing more than the measure of a shadow, never stationary, but lengthening as the sun advances, and to be taken anew from hour to hour."

But on one thing about Virginia, you and I and Jefferson would agree. We love it.

CONTENTS

'THIS STET...SO GRET'

On venturing beyond the borders of this Eden we call Virginia, you have noticed, I'm sure, how those in other states manage, sooner or later, to work into the conversation a tie, if only a ribbon, to Virginia.

Not far along in the talk, a person will say: We came through there in '46. (1846, it turns out.)

Or, I was there during the war.

Or, we have kin in Virginia. (Cousins, thrice removed.)

Once, in a company where the discoveries of Virginia connections went on and on, around the circle, one poor fellow sat silent, with no claim to call his own, it seemed, until finally, unable to stand it any longer, he burst out: Well, I HAD MY APPENDIX TAKEN OUT IN VIRGINIA!

It was, as they say, a stopper.

But there's no end to the variety of Virginians.

When someone identified General Douglas MacArthur as a native of Arkansas, he set the matter straight in a good-natured but firm affirmation.

"It was intended," he said, "that I be born in Virginia, my mother's home."

Thus, with a grand casualness, he reordered events in which he couldn't take a hand 83 years before when his father, an army man, was assigned suddenly to Little Rock.

A Virginian by intent!

(Norfolk changed its old Courthouse into an impressive memorial for the Old Soldier. If the General became one of the elect by edict, his gentle, dark-eyed wife slipped quietly in and out of the city—and into its heart—without trying.)

Another West Pointer was more diffident in advancing his credentials.

"I am a Virginian," said Edgar Allan Poe, "or at least I call myself one."

Poe needn't have fretted. Virginia is not behind in recognizing her own, even an Israfel, once they win renown.

Amid pawn shops and second-hand stores on East Main Street in Richmond, the Poe Shrine is a charming retreat, filled with curios of the sort to intrigue Poe, which I first visited as a high school student.

Was Edgar Allan Poe born here? I asked the hostess.

No, she said. He was born in Boston.

Did he die here?

He died in Baltimore.

Did the Raven come to him here?

No. But, she added firmly, I think we can safely say that from time to time *he must have passed by!*

And, in passing, left some haunting poetry.

On his way to the pawnshops.

Politicians who were born elsewhere have devised their own category: by-choice Virginians.

"My opponent," they will say, "could not help it. He was born in Virginia. But, ladies and gentlemen, I am different. I came to this beloved state of my own will. *I AM A VIRGINIAN BY CHOICE!*"

In one notable instance, Virginians found an old school tie with a politician. When the Old Dominion's delegates caucused at the 1956

2

Democratic national convention in Chicago to pick a Vice-Presidential nominee, they knew too much about Senator Kefauver to suit their conservative taste and too little about young Kennedy, the Eagle Scout, golden in the kleig lights.

Then someone remembered he'd heard that the young man from Massachusetts had a brother who had gone to the law school at the Unicersity of Virginia. That did it. The Virginians went whooping out to the convention hall to support the Brother of a Cavalier.

Many of us become Virginians by marrying Virginians.

I was born in Georgia, we say (or any other of the states), *BUT*, we add, hastily, *MY WIFE* (or husband) *IS A VIRGINIAN!*

In much the same way, I expect my wife to pull me across the sill of heaven.

John Jasper, the famous evangelist who spent his life half-slaved, half-free, had a word on Virginia as a state of bliss.

There are four races of men, Mr. Jasper told his flock. the Aborigines, the Hottentots, the Abyssinians, and the Virginians.

And Virginians, he said, are the only race that doesn't have to be born again.

What is it—and I put the question to you frankly, without shoeing around the sumac—what is it that makes us so great?

Or gret, as the Virginians, especially the politicians, say.

3

(And, while I am thinking about it, what makes the politicians say gret, this GRET Commonwealth, the GRET Patrick Henry, and so on. Perhaps because somehow it makes things twice as great, to say gret. There's more awe, more incredulity in gret, an exclamatory word that spreads its arms wide and falls over backward at the grandeur of what it is describing.)

All right then, what makes this stet so gret?

What is it about Virginia?

There is the name.

Virginia. . .

It sings itself.

When an overseer, addressing a letter, dared to write "Va.", John Randolph of Roanoke snatched the letter, tore it up, and shouted:

" 'Va.'! Damn your 'Va.' !"

He wanted every precious syllable saved: Vir-gin-i-a.

And no wonder.

The very land is in the name.

In the sweet, undulating roll of Virginia, you can catch the soft folds of the Blue Ridge mountains in the morning mist, the giddy, gaudy green Easter Egg hills billowing around Albemarle, the lazy James embracing Richmond, the dark green tobacco fields somnolent in the Southside sun, and the long, pale green combers rolling in white thunder on Virginia Beach.

The geography, too, seems to nurture the nature of the people.

The major rivers rise and make their way to the Chesapeake Bay without ever leaving Virginia.

They know.

Why leave? they ask. Life is good around us.

The contour of the State offers every scenery—seacoast, tidewater, piedmont, mountains—as if to say, beguilingly, stay, it's all here, all that earth can afford.

Even the mountains are moderate.

They are old mountains, mellowed by time and the weather, grandfathers offering a knee to children.

None is too steep to climb of a Sunday. The benign, smiling Blue Ridge, under the full glare of the mid-day sun, has a trick of almost fading away into nothingness, becoming part and parcel of the azure air, atomizing before your very eyes, a wispy, lightly-patterned veil rather than a wall, as if you could see through its mountains, much like those into which the Pied Piper disappeared.

In *Notes on the State of Virginia,* Thomas Jefferson said that Natural Bridge was "the most sublime of nature's works."

And yet it slips up on you.

As it did on me when I left a convention of newspapermen late one afternoon in December and walked, or skidded, down a winding path between two mountain walls white with snow. At a turn in the path along the creek was a large sign noting the height of the bridge, 215 feet; the width, 50 to 150 feet, and the length, 90 feet. I was moving along the path, wondering how much farther the bridge was, when, looking up, I saw it hanging in the sky, so high that I'd been looking straight through it without even seeing it, while it looked down, smiling, on me.

With me were a colleague's two daughters, Jennie and Julie Daffron. You all seen this bridge before? I asked, awed.

Julie nodded. It's always larger than you remember, she said.

It is so large, so various, that looking at one part you feel that another is escaping you, and you keep turning and backing away, as if viewing a revolving panorama of rock, trees, sky, and the creek that carved it.

Unlike some massive formations, the bridge has an airiness, a buoyancy in its soaring height, that lifts instead of oppresses. It bears lightly a multitude of details and history. In Colonial times soldiers dropped molten lead from its top into the creek to make bullets. Today a highway runs atop it without many travelers realizing they are speeding across its broad back.

A young surveyor, George Washington, climbed 23 feet up one wall and carved his initials. The insatiable Jefferson did even more. He bought the bridge from King George III for 20 shillings and built a log cabin for visitors, the first Virginian (as with nearly everything) to think of luring tourists.

With Jefferson, however, it was not a desire to make money, but to spread enlightenment. He couldn't resist an idea (had a "canine appetite", he said, for learning) and couldn't rest until he had shared it with the rest of the world. His log cabin had a book in which visitors might write their impressions of the Great Bridge.

Trees peeping over the top of the bridge are reduced in size to clumps of mistletoe. Five-foot icicles hang from the roof, like long white goatees. In severe winters they attain a length of 14 feet and have to be blasted away with a shotgun, said our guide.

I walked under the granite dome and out onto the other side of the bridge, and backed along, looking up at it. Suddenly, at a turn in the walkway, it was as if a granite door had shut, and left nothing but the rugged face of the cliff. I edged forward a yard or so, and a jagged patch of light appeared in the rock face, and then another pace brought the streak of light wider and deeper, as in a dagger stroke, as if the rock were splitting, and two more strides disclosed the full gate-way.

From the first approach, the bridge is on you, towering complete, before you know it; coming back, you catch it in stages as if the cliff were being sundered dramatically.

The first to see the bridge were Indians, Monocans, legend says, who stumbled upon it as a way to cross the canyon and escape from pursuing Shawnees and Powhatans.

Are any Indians left around here? I asked our guide.

The only one he'd seen, said the guide, was an Indian tourist who had come down in the gorge and eyed the bridge for a long time.

What did he say?

He said it looked to him like something the white man planned and the Indian dug.

7

HOW STURDY IS SHORT PUMP

"Heaven and earth never agreed better to frame a place for man's habitation," wrote John Smith, trying to win recruits to the New World. "Here are hills, plains, valleys, rivers and brooks, all running most pleasantly into a faire bay encompassed about with fruitful and delightsome land."

And in the names they give this fruitful and delightsome land, the Virginians pay it homage.

They bestow the names on places and things as casually, as airily, as lovingly as Adam and Eve walking about the Garden, saying "There's a soanso!", and, sure enough, there it is, and it could have been nothing else.

In his book on names across the nation, George R. Stewart wrote: "Most important of all, the Virginians had no policy or system of naming so that their names from the beginning grew more naturally, and were more adapted to the country, and more various. Even their names of towns and counties sprang rather from the people than from the government. For these reasons there was no marked cleavage between such names and those of natural features. . . ."

Sweet Chalybeate, but he's right!

Not to mention Haysi (named for a general store run by Hayter and Sypher).

Or Oilville, Central Garage, and Motorun.

When the Board of Supervisors of Pittsylvania County rechristened a community with the new name of Fairview, the residents rebelled. They wanted the old name: Tightsqueeze.

So the supervisors reversed themselves. But it was a tight squeeze for Tightsqueeze.

The wild things still fly, creep, and crawl on the road signs, if not the roadsides.

(And passing Bear Wallow, with just a glimpse of the highway marker in the headlights' glare, the motorist wonders if a bear isn't out there yet, shadowy, ghost-like, moseying, mud-bedraggled out of the Wallow.)

There's Coonseye, shining in the darkness, too, and Buzzard's Roost, Buffalo Gap, Turkey Knob, Rabbit Run, Wolftrap, Raccoon Ford, and strayed from the farm, Pig Point.

There is also Stingray Point where Captain John Smith stepped on a stingray, and, outraged and vainglorious—it was surely the most important thing that had happened that day—named it in anger for the creature that stung him there.

And there are all the Indian names, full of acorns pelting the frost-hard earth, the spring wind sweeping through the pussy-willows, croaking frogs, the whir and smack of an arrow, and all the howling night wilderness . . . Accomac, Piankatank, Shenandoah, Massanutten, Powhatan, and Zuni still stalking the land, wraith-like, in feathered fierceness.

Is Zuni an Indian name, I wonder?

If it ain't, it ought to be.

But, indubitably, the crossroads of Pungo near Virginia Beach is named for an Indian chief, although how the braves addressed their sachem without doubling up with laughter is a wonder.

Chuckatuck, close to Suffolk, is named, according to legend, for two chiefs, Chuck and Tuck, each of whom desired to leave his brand on the land, and so the chiefs compromised on an amalgam, in the manner of such corporations as Desilu. Nothing is new. (An alternative, as enticing, is that Chuckatuck was a Colonial colloquialism meaning chockablock.)

There's the Mattaponi River, and, as you drive along Interstate 95, there come running across the road to mama:
the Matta,
    the Po,
        and the Ni,

three branches, or creeks, like baby 'possums, hanging on their mother's tail.

Then there's the town that turned Indian to become a city.

When the Norfolk and Western Railroad brought prospects of prosperity to Big Lick, its proud citizens named the place Roanoke, Indian for wampum.

But you can still find Paint Lick, Water Lick, and Mudlick Junction, if you look.

The railroads left their mark elsewhere, too. William Mahone, the Confederate General who became a Republican after the war, owned the Atlantic, Mississippi, and Ohio Railroad (predecessor of the N&W), and one day he and his wife Otelia rode down the line naming the stations from her favorite novels by Sir Walter Scott: Ivor, Windsor, Wakefield, and Waverly, until finally they got to a spot on which they couldn't agree, and called it Disputanta. The people took a hand in the game of naming too. They said that the General's railroad, the AM&O, stood for All Mine and Otelia's.

The town of La Crosse was christened, legend relates, by a work crew building a railroad. The workmen came bang up against the rails of a rival line and asked their boss what to do.

"Do?" he shouted. "Why, lay cross! Lay cross!"

The injunction prevailed at the junction.

One of the great name droppers was Colonel William Byrd II. On a trip through the wilderness he named a couple of places that weren't there, as he relates in his diary of 1733:

"We laid the foundation of two large cities. One at Shacco's to be called Richmond, and the other at the point of the Appomattox River to be named Petersburg. . . . Thus we did not build castles only, but also cities in the air."

There are puzzlers like Non Intervention, Skinquarter (named, perhaps, for a nearby spring at which Indians skinned and quartered game), Rip Raps, Summerduck, and Short Pump.

G. Watson James, Jr., who aided in editing *Virginia Historical Portraiture,* likes to tell of the Virginian who listed his place of residence, simply, grandly, as Short Pump.

Anybody ought to know where Short Pump is.

The settlement, between Charlottesville and Richmond, was named for

Short Pump Tavern, and that in turn took its name from the pump under the porch. How eminently sensible to pin a locality's tag on somebody or something. Even when the meaning is lost in time's dust, it piques the imagination. How sturdy is Short Pump. How much more abiding than Celestial Acres or Elysian Fields.

The name grew there with the pump, and it is a point in time, saying here we were, laughing, and drinking, and clattering through the place in our boots, and tramping about in the mud around the pump.

And, finally, there's Begood.

I know how that must have started, with women saying good-by interminably, calling forever in the dusk: "Now be good, hear? . . . You all be good! . . . You be good, too . . . We will, and don't you all forget to be good . . .", over and over, until finally some impatient husband called it, in desperation, Begood.

And, perhaps, Begone!

A visitor can find Virginians exceedingly vague, but they know full well what they mean, most of the time, when they say The Beach, The Tearoom, The Woman's Club, The River (though there are a dozen) and The University (to the annoyance of alumni of the universities, although they, too, fall in line in conversation.)

Richmonders speak of the Wrong Side of Broad Street, which happens to be the north side, but the direction has nothing to do with the designation. Strangers are at a loss to define the difference between the two sides, and many natives can't put it into words, knowing only that as children they felt a nameless apprehension when they walked down the Wrong Side, as if they were suddenly alone and exposed under an alien sky, all the more wary because they did not know why, and did not feel at ease until they had crossed the street and gained the shadow of the comfortable bulk of Miller and Rhoads or Thalhimers.

A scholar dug into this taboo and discovered in the City Directory of 1892 a listing of 25 saloons on the north side of Broad Street and only three on the south side. The saloons have vanished but their fame and the name remain.

There is that song, possibly the most evocative of the state anthems.

James Bland, composer of minstrel songs, stood in the doorway of his kitchen in Washington, D. C., and watched, listened, and noted as an old woman, a former slave, sat before a fire and yearned with a exile's longing of home:

Carry me back to ole Virginny . . .

There is the soft talk, the drawl that is not quite a drawl and touches only certain words.

It is frustrating to try to put them on paper in all their caressing sound, as if the speaker loved the words so much that he was reluctant to let them go without a quick kiss or pat on the head, simple words like out (ow-oo-ut), house (how-oos). . .

Some Virginians have a fine, casual way of strewing y's around, dropping one into garden (gyarden), or the car (cyah).

Only in Virginia does a "gyuard" play on the "vyarsity." And the simple past becomes the wondrous "pair-uhst," rooted far back in England. It is no more put on than the ivy clinging to the church tower at Jamestown.

Generally, it is the short words on which Virginians dwell so lovingly, a selective drawl that does not wind unending on the nerves but catches you by surprise on only certain words.

The way my wife says bird.

The up and down of it, like a wild canary flying. The word becomes the bird, and takes wing: buh-er-r-r-r-r-r-r-r-u-u-u-dd-d-d-duh. To make

it accurate, I'd have to stretch it all the way across the page and back.

The other day she started to say there's a bird on the back fence, and when she hit the first buh sound I went in the kitchen for a drink of water and when I got back she had just hit duh, and the bird had flown away, built a nest, hatched its young, come back, caught a worm and was feeding it to a fledgling on the fence. It was a robin.

Yard lengthens itself into "yah-uhd," becoming almost an estate in the process. And that cold, narrow-eyed, Northern word "hard" is softened into "hah-uhd," as if spoken languidly from a hammock about something that has to be done day after tomorrow, if at all.

Gracing the soft talk are the sweet courtesies in a land where men still say sir (or suh) and ma'am (even when one party is all of 40 and the other no more than 50), and doff their hats in elevators, and give up seats to women on buses, and open doors for them, and take their arms in crossing the street—and are surprised when visitors are surprised at these amenities.

ALL SEASONS, PLUS ONE

Virginia is a state for all seasons, but none is extreme. Each lasts only long enough to leave the wish it had lasted a little longer. Even the winter has benign stretches, an old man dreaming by the fire of the days of his youth.

Begin with the autumn because even more than the visionary spring September is a season of business-like beginnings, of going back to classes, of going back to work after summer vacation, of going back to Sunday school and church and finding the preacher still there, a resumption of responsibilities, a renewing of duties.

The fall recalls the Blue Ridge Mountains and proud Chief Logan of the Mingo Indians. He was a friend of the settlers, even when the other Indians fought them, until white men ambushed and killed all his family and provoked Logan to war. When peace was restored, the great chief responded to Governor Dunmore with an oration which Thomas Jefferson rated with the best of Demosthenes and Cicero. It concluded:

"For my country, I rejoice at the beams of peace. But do not harbor a thought that mine is the joy of fear. Logan never felt fear. He will not turn on his heel to save his life. Who is there to mourn for Logan? Not one."

In the fall the slopes of the Blue Ridge throng with jostling tribes of trees in blazing war bonnets—yellow hickory, flaming maple, bronze and purple oaks—and the broom sage fields along the Valley floor are dotted with dark green scrub pines, crouching scouts sent out ahead of the multitude of warriors carpeting the mountains, descending in an aura of color.

They come, I think, to mourn Logan.

Snow comes seldom enough in a Virginia winter, so that the first child to see the first snow bounds into the room shouting, "It snowed!", and you look out on a world gift-wrapped in white and feel the old excitement.

In a Virginia snowstorm, which is anything more than an inch of snow, the Virginia housewife doesn't feel secure until she has a loaf of bread in the house, or an extra loaf if she already has one.

Going down to the corner to fetch the staff of life in the white, silent world of the most recent storm, I found the baker, also in white, a hefty fellow, in furious motion, like an agitated snowman, trying to move his white truck, jumping in and out of it, shoving and pushing at it, as if he were biffing and baffing a big batch of dough on the way to being a loaf. "This," he said, looking around at the freshly-iced world, "is one of 'em."

Virginians take snow to heart. Inside the bakery the lady behind the counter said she'd never have made it but for the dairyman's bringing her out, as if she'd been in the Adirondacks. And the clerk from the drugstore, which hadn't opened, came in to use the bakery phone and announced to somebody: "I got here!", as if she'd landed on Mars. All of us are adventurers in the snow. I bore home the bread like Jason.

The great thing about snow is the way it singularizes. Driving from Norfolk to Richmond later that day, I passed a crow, sitting atop the snow in a field close to the road, and you never saw such a crow-like crow. He was not simply a crow; he was the crow. Regardez the crow! C-R-O-W, as if in a child's primer. Or the first crow ever invented, and set aside a moment while the creator pondered whether to strike the model and populate the earth and the skies thereof with crows, and maybe throw in a few white ones for sea gulls, or smash it, and start over. The crowness of that crow, a dark exclamation mark on the white backdrop, was a triumph. Without his opening his beak, his presence cawed blackly in the white silence.

A little farther, a flock of smaller birds—starlings or grackles—raced for cover, chased by a big, bluish-headed hawk, his wings beating in slow, powerful oar-strokes, a policeman scattering hoodlums. It was cheering, the sudden notice in the snow, that amid civilization's steadily macadamizing crawl, a hawk could still prowl.

A train came along, a coal carrier, and, lo, the gondola cars were heaped in white, as if the commercial-minded old C&O had gotten into the swing of things and was exuberantly hauling snow all about the landscape. And at the next annual meeting, some prissy stockholder would arise and say: Mr. Chairman, what is the explanation of this day in which all the cars were on the road, coming and going, but there was no coal hauled? Is that any way to run a railroad?

And the Chairman would reply, meekly, that some of the boys thought it would be a lark if we hauled snow all day, and, at the time, it seemed a good idea, and it was quite-a-sight.

Nature provides nothing higher in Tidewater than a dune at Seashore State Park, but children all along Interstate 64 had discovered the big man-made pyramids at the overpasses. Each steep side had its complement of sleigh-riders, and dogs bounding sideways after them.

Each sight was a temptation to stop, and, finally, on the Richmond side of Williamsburg, was a stand of tall pines, an experiment in controlled cutting by a lumber company, that could not be resisted. At first glance, as the car approached, their massed, dark-brown trunks seemed a wood-paneled corridor along the road.

But viewed head-on, the pine forest was an enormous room steeped in dark green gloom, except where the snow had sifted through and caught in patches on the bark, and on short, broken stubs along the tall trunks, and when the sun came out, and picked out the thousands of dazzling white spots in the dark cave, it was as if the passerby had been offered a look into the human heart.

The first sign of spring in Virginia is the changing of the light, as dramatic as the changing of the guard at Buckingham Palace, only subtler. Even without going out, even before getting up in the morning, almost without having to open your eyes, you can tell spring is in Virginia. The branches out the window are as bare, but the light that plays over them has a promise, as if the light itself would blossom shortly.

A little later spring comes on boldly and the air is rife with life. Every square inch is bursting with activity, yodeling with glee, right down to a tiny green-gold bee, blazing like an emerald. Sweat bees, we used to call them.

But none of the fanfare can equal that first light.

Many count the summer incomplete that does not include a day or two at Virginia Beach.

Virginia Beach is the main street of Virginia. Stroll any nine blocks along its slightly sloping width, and you find friends from as many places, scattered in whorls around beach umbrellas as if swept there by the tides. It is a reunion by the sea.

The beach is crunchy as broken snow near the boardwalk, sifted flour-soft near the middle, and hard-packed as a brown fist nearing the water's edge. The ocean, too, comes in bands, violet at the horizon, almost blending with the light-filled sky; turning to deep blue a little lower as it secures its own domain; then green, nearing shore, and, finally, taking on a golden tint as it shakes out in rolling white combers on the brown sand of the beach.

But the chief attraction is the scope it offers anybody to play as a child, or even a fool. You cannot simply run for fun along a downtown street, at least not without pretending to chase a bus, nor can you sit down and construct a castle on the curb, even if there were sand, instead of the city's detritus. But almost any antic is accepted on the beach.

Crouching a moment under an on-gathering breaker, just before it breaks, hearing the rustling waters at its brim, smelling the slightly sour seaweed, you find it easy to understand that the first life came from the sea. And viewing the wide blue plain from a dune, you think of a Virginian, Matthew Fontaine Maury, beginning his treatise on the Gulf Stream in grand, Genesis-like simplicity: "There is a river in the ocean."

It is a grand note on which to end a survey of the four seasons in Virginia, but there is a fifth, a season-in-between, and I learned about it when a friend stood near my typewriter and looked out the window and said he had the sandpiper blues.

It's the time of year, he explained, when the sandpipers are appearing on the beach. They fly in tight formations, like thrown jackrocks, and land just at the water's edge, all in a close-strung flock, and skitter across the sand, tiny birds running in and out with the waves, so fragile and quick that sometimes when you blink your eyes, they vanish. When I first see them about mid-August, he said, I know that the season is changing. And after they come in numbers, the people leave, and the beach is a brown, bare stage, waiting.

It's a restless time for everybody, he said. The children, now that summer is gone, are wild to grab every precious minute in the waning sun, and yet their minds are on school, too, because their mothers are herding them to the dentist and goading them into finishing their summer reading lists, which they haven't started.

Even the sun is uncertain and has a faint, cidery, fall look to it, amberish, ambiguous; and the sky is fretful, somehow hurried and remote, as if someone is changing scenery, not at all like the hot, still skies of July, and there's a tinge, just a breath of autumn in the air.

You're tired of summer clothes, he said, and yet it's too early for fall wear. The songs on the car radio about summer are old hat, but, as is our way with old hats, we hate to let them go.

I wish, he said, spinning around, I wish I could spend the days between August 15 and September 15 on a long vacation, away from this season in between. It's really a thirteenth month, which I'd like to skip. Soon autumn will be with us with its tonic air and antics, but right now I've got the sandpiper blues.

He started to leave, but at the door he paused and said: Write about it. Let everybody else be miserable with me. And put a name to Virginia's thirteenth month.

We checked here and there for suggestions, and at last ,a 12-year-old, who had done his summer reading, proposed: Name it for the Greek god of change: Proteus.

There it is then; *June, July, August, Proteus, September. . .*

THE HOUSE OF OUR FATHERS

To startling degree, the homes of great Virginians reflect their characters much as Frank Lloyd Wright's dictum—"Form follows function"—suggested that a building should be a continuum of its setting and purpose. The founding fathers' dwelling places not only are indigenous to the landscape; they declare the inner men, as surely as the shell of a turtle or the nest of the mockingbird.

Monticello with its dome and balanced wings mirrors the cool, classical Greek mould of Jefferson's thought. To go through the rooms and come upon the gadgets, like the cannonball clock over the doorway, is to wander through Jefferson's inventive mind.

"All my wishes end, where I hope my life will end, at Monticello," said Jefferson.

In Montpelier there's a symmetry that you find in the checks and balances structured into the Constitution by the "great little Madison" (as his Dolly-to-be wrote of him to a friend when she heard he first was coming to call) and the expanse of the lawn reflects the breadth of his thought. He terraced his garden in a horseshoe amphitheater along the lines of the Hall of the House of Representatives.

The Republic was never far from the center of his thinking. In a note found after his death, he urged his countrymen: "The advice nearest to my heart and deepest in my conviction is that the Union of the States be cherished and perpetuated. Let the open enemy of it be regarded as a Pandora with her box opened, and the disguised one as the serpent creeping with his deadly wiles into Paradise."

He and Jefferson worked as a team guiding State and national affairs, which often were one and the same, with Virginia a proving ground for ideas applied in Washington. Those two, and others, dared to be philosophers. The nation flourished not because the founders did what seemed easy or even practical immediately, but because they were visionaries and boldly demanded the ideal. The areas of tragic failure in our history— where the nation has had to retrace its way painfully for a fresh start— are precisely the points where the framers of the Constitution and members of Congress declined to go along with the plans of the Great Speculators. The most fearful lapse was with the issue of slavery. Treating the subject in his *Notes on the State of Virginia*, Jefferson wrote that he trembled for his country when he reflected that God is just.

Madison understood only too well the difficulties of writing a Constitution that would withstand "the silent innovations of time on the meaning of words and phrasing." But the probe of his mind is still arching beyond us on some issues. So abrupt and deep a separation did he wish for church and state that he opposed presidential proclamations of prayer.

With them and a handful of others, the nation was their own creation, personal and deeply-felt, as much as a work of art to a sculptor or a child to the mother. They withheld nothing from the cause. Near the close, to survive, Jefferson sold his beloved library to Congress. Dolly, after Jamie's death, was forced to sell Montpelier. Their reward was their country's welfare. Their grand experiment worked.

The serene brow of Mount Vernon overlooking the Potomac is a happy statement of George Washington's character. It tells volumes, as does the portrait of the master of the house by Gilbert Stuart. The viewer has the sense of being in the presence of majesty.

What comes through strongly in Stuart's study is the calm stamina that outlasted Valley Forge and the British and the vexations of his own vital, excitable fellow Americans. Among his contentious contemporaries, he was the arbiter. At times, indeed, they seemed to agree only in their trust of Washington and his absolute commitment to moral right.

In the long, sheep-like face, the straight, firm mouth, the slightly sloe eyes, and the triangular wedges of white hair, there is something of the Sphinx, and fellow patriots — the various Jefferson, tart Adams, imperious Hamilton, moderate Madison, merry Franklin, resourceful Marshall—clambered, worshipful as boys, about his great paws. In the sands of time, Washington stays.

Some lament that photography was not invented soon enough to fix his features. But no stiff, congealing daguerreotype could reproduce the whole man as Stuart did—formidable, but warm; slightly forbidding, but a man on whom always you could rely. No wonder his countrymen called him father.

*   *   *   *

In the lovely home of George Mason, exquisite in detail, you find an intensely private man forever recalled to some duty in public life, but he wrote his concern for the privacy and dignity of the individual into the Virginia Declaration of Rights as carefully as he saw to the carpentering of Gunston Hall.

The home might be called a valentine since Mason supervised its building for his 16-year-old bride, Ann Eilbeck of Maryland's Eastern Shore. The builder, William Buckland, was a master craftsman from Oxfordshire, England. Gunston Hall was his first commission in America.

Gunston Hall appears to be a mansion in miniature, but the modest appearance is deceptive. Its story-and-a-half housed the Masons and their nine offspring comfortably, and it was a center of Virginia hospitality at its best. A frequent visitor from neighboring Mount Vernon was George Washington. The two Georges swapped conversation and cuttings from fruit trees.

Women visitors today take special delight in Gunston Hall. Although they find it difficult to picture themselves in such baronial places as Stratford and Carter's Grove, Gunston Hall seems within reach of their dreams.

The center of the formal gardens is an aisle of 200-year-old boxwoods twice as tall as a man, extending 200 feet. The narrow way seems to be carved out of dark green jade and from that corridor of foliage the visitor steps out on a mound, like a rostrum, and looks down on a deer park and beyond to the Potomac River. Deer still run there and eagles rise above Mason's Neck, one of their few remaining nesting places along the river.

In Gunston Hall's Little Sitting Room is the small table on which Mason drafted the Virginia Declaration of Rights with its grand opening proclaiming "That all men are by nature equally free and independent, and have certain inherent rights . . . namely, the enjoyment of life and liberty, with the means of acquiring and possessing property and obtaining happiness and safety."

His Declaration of Rights influenced Jefferson's phrasing of the Declaration of Independence and formed the basis of the U. S. Constitution's Bill of Rights.

In Article 15 Mason's Declaration warns "that no free government can be preserved . . . but by frequent recurrence to fundamental principles." Politicians love to roll "the frequent recurrence" on their tongues; it is sound advice, unless, in looking back, we become mesmerized with past glories and forget to move ahead, guided by the fundamental principles.

Ann died after they had been married 23 years, and George Mason's heart was in his pen as he wrote her epitaph:

> *Once she was all that cheers and sweetens life*
> *The tender mother, daughter, friend, and wife.*
> *Once she was all that makes mankind adore,*
> *Now view this marble and be vain no more.*

*   *   *   *

And look at John Marshall's home in Richmond, plain and unadorned, four-square sturdy as the builder. Marshall, more than any man after Washington, was responsible for putting the national government on a strong footing. "I went into the army a Virginian," he said, "and came out an American."

His house used to share the block with a high school, but, since 1962, it stands stubtoed beneath a monolithic cliff of a Federal office building. There's dramatic cause and effect between the little house on the corner and the spreading Federal structure behind it. That pile of masonry might perturb Marshall, but he wasn't a man to scare easy, or for long.

He worked until he was 80 at his Court and Constitution and died while on a trip to Philadelphia. As the people bore his body along the streets to the dock to go home to Virginia, the Liberty Bell tolled from Independence Hall, and in ringing for John Marshall, the bell cracked, as if a job was done.

His portion was finished, but the contending strains — Marshall's Federalism v. Jefferson's State Rights — are as vital as when the two cousins warred over them; and the solution is not the utter defeat of either but in the continuing contending. Indeed, on varying issues, the battleground can shift in the same mind and man, as it did with Jefferson's pushing the Ordinance of 1784 to prohibit slavery, nullification and secession in the new Northwest Territory.

*   *   *   *

To come nearer in time, go to Stratford, the birthplace of Lee in

Westmoreland County—solid, massive, self-reliant, a couchant lion, enigmatic in its simplicity. The man from that home could take hammer blows and not crack.

After the war, to an aide who told of discontented veterans, Lee replied: "Tell them that they must all set to work, and if they cannot do what they prefer, do what they can. Virginia wants all their aid, all their support, and the presence of all her sons to sustain and recuperate her."

Thus, he overcame even the swarming might-have-beens.

*   *   *   *

At Washington and Lee is a statue to Cyrus McCormick,
Which notes, among other things, he "liberated agriculture,"
And 20 miles away is Walnut Grove,
Where in 1831 he invented the reaper,
Which, when he moved to Chicago, nearer the wheatfields,
Helped the North feed its armies, and trade with Britain, for much-needed gold,
And the heirs of Cyrus gave Walnut Grove to VPI
Which operates it as a research station
For liberating agriculture,
Among other things.

*   *   *   *

"I was born a slave on a plantation in Franklin County," is the opening of Booker T. Washington's *Up from Slavery*. His home was a log

cabin, about 14 by 16 feet. The National Park Service experienced little difficulty duplicating it.

His quest for education for himself and his people is a story to stand with Benjamin Franklin's *Autobiography*. In his first brush with schooling after the war, he saw during the roll call that "Booker" was not enough, and when the teacher asked his name, he replied calmly, "Washington."

Working in a West Virginia coal mine, he heard two miners talking about "a great school for colored people somewhere in Virginia." Begging rides and walking, he started the 500-mile trek to Hampton Institute. Exhausted and penniless in Richmond, he spent several nights beneath a board sidewalk, under the tramping of feet, and worked by day loading pig iron on a boat.

Hampton's head teacher, pondering what to do with him, told him to sweep a recitation room. He swept it three times. Then he got a dusting cloth and dusted it four times — the woodwork, every bench, table, and desk. When the teacher failed to find a speck of dirt, she said quietly, "I guess you will do for this institution."

The book is marked by fortitude, sweetness of spirit, and a grave humor. I got into it belatedly when I heard my seventh grader laughing with delight at Booker T.'s account of his bout with his bed at Hampton: "The sheets were quite a puzzle to me. The first night I slept under both of them, and the second night I slept on top of both of them; but by watching the other boys I learned my lesson in this and have been trying to follow it ever since and teach it to others."

In mid-20th century, some civil rights leaders dismissed him as an "Uncle Tom," and some patrons of at least one Booker T. Washington High School were defensive about it. The name is a proud one in which all should glory.

I talked with his daughter in Washington, D. C., Portia Washington Pittman, a witty, charming little woman of 83, direct as a child, and yet motherly toward her father who worked himself to death at 56.

"People looked to him for advice everywhere," she said. "The poor man couldn't take it all. He'd wake up nights sick. He died of hypertension."

Catching a train could become a trial, she said, as when he called a hack to hurry to a station in the Deep South.

"We don't haul no niggers down here!" said the driver.

"You get in the back, and let me haul you," said Booker T.

His daughter smiled and said: "He knew that the main thing was to get things adjusted, and he wanted both races to work together."

He was far ahead in advocating job training, she said, and he told his people "to get an education and learn a trade and begin a business and get money in the bank. He told them to get ready. I think they are beginning to appreciate him."

She sat on the sofa in a back hallway room, and although she was heavy with age, there was a gay air of a pleased child in her smile and intent eyes, so that she seemed to be sitting very straight, the petite Portia that her father liked to have around. "He said I rested him," she said.

"He made me learn sewing. I hated it. I didn't care about anything but my music. . . But for his sake I got a certificate from the dressmaking department at Tuskegee. My daughter will tell you I can't sew a seam.

"I don't know where I got that music from, but I didn't care for that old industrial stuff." The daughter of Booker T. Washington, who had cleaned a room three times at Hampton, laughed and said: "I couldn't clean up my room right. My father realized when I was small that music was my forte, and I studied in Europe with a pupil of Franz Liszt."

Near the end of the interview, she said, "When you first called, I thought you were a Negro. I have to be very guarded. I wondered why any Negro would be so interested in my father. That's what puzzled me."

She had attended the dedication of the center in Franklin County— "Hasn't God been good to me to let me see it?" — and had accepted an invitation to speak at nearby Ferrum College.

"I'm going to talk about my daddy, what else? Tell 'em what that little slave boy from Franklin County did."

*   *   *   *

"A man's rootage is more important than his fruitage," said Woodrow Wilson, and his roots are in Staunton at the Manse, rectangular in its rectitude, breeding ground for a Covenanter for whom were no grays, only black and white. It's all there in his birthplace, prim, precise, and Presbyterian.

Woodrow Wilson was born in the 12-room house of white brick in 1856. His father, Dr. Joseph Ruggles Wilson, preached in the church

down the street and taught at Mary Baldwin College, then the Augusta Female Seminary, across the way. Young Wilson lived there nearly a year and returned several times.

On December 12, 1912, President-elect Wilson stayed overnight in the room in which he was born. All his life he said, emphatically, he was a Virginian and associated himself with those of the long view: Washington, Jefferson, Madison, Mason.

In the Manse is the cradle which rocked him, and rocked, too, the beginnings of an ideal of a world governed by reason that will persist.

*　　*　　*　　*

On high land, overlooking the Staunton River near Brookneal, is Red Hill, the last home and the burial place of that restless spirit, Patrick Henry.

The house had to be reconstructed, but Henry's law office still stands, as does a majestic osage orange tree. Its limbspread measures 90 feet, its trunk's circumference is 23 feet, and its diameter is 9 feet. It is 50 feet tall and between 250 and 300 years old.

The original flagstone walk leads to the family graveyard and Henry's tomb, on which is inscribed: "His fame his best epitaph."

On summer evenings Henry gathered his numerous family around him beneath the osage orange and entertained them with his fiddle and flute. It was a quiet scene with which to close a turbulent life. But there was one final flare for the old orator. In 1799, at George Washington's urging, the ailing Henry took two days to travel 20 miles to Charlotte County Courthouse. There he made his last speech in defense of the Union in a debate with John Randolph at Roanoke. That was a cosmic clash, between a rising and a falling star, as they had it out over the nature of Federalism.

*   *   *   *

When a Virginia politician speaks of "the House of Our Fathers"— which he is either about to bolt, or bolt shut—he customarily is a Democrat referring to the National Democratic Party, but the symbol arising in his and his hearers' minds is the State House designed by Thomas Jefferson from the Maison Carrée in France.

The Republicans also regard it firmly as their home, although presently in the minority, and so do the squirrels and the pigeons and the secretaries who come from all sides of the Square at noon to lunch on the lawn.

That is a fetching sight — the gray-looming, great-columned structure at the top of the slope and scattered on the green lawn beneath its guardian wings the girls in their bright frocks, their skirts spread about them flaring on the lawn like vivid circular beds of phlox.

(Once some loungers in the sun on the benches along the walks addressed uncouth, if complimentary, remarks to the passing secretaries. The reaction of the Keepers of the Square was swift, if roundabout: they took out all the benches. To paint them, they said.

(That took care of the loafers.

(And grim no-trespass signs sprouted on the slopes. To save the grass they said.

(That excluded the girls.

(Then, gradually, the signs disappeared, and the girls came back, twittering, and the benches reappeared, repainted, and the loafers returned, repentant, and all was right in the Square.)

That is a long parenthesis, but the parenthetical is important in Virginia. Many a crisis is averted by solving it as something else, (parenthetically).

The last time I passed through the Square, an entire many-membered family of tourists was picnicking beneath the gray gaze of the South Portico—not a discreet sandwich or two but an all-out dinner on the grounds, a red-checked tablecloth under a parasol, with jars of preserves, and crocks of pickles, and a tall, multi-layer chocolate cake, a feast fit for Renoir's "The Luncheon of the Boating Party"

THE PAST, WITHOUT APOLOGIES

The oyster gray House on the Hill doesn't belong to either political party, but to the people, which would please Jefferson. Appropriately, the most distinguished resident of the Square is the Father of His Country—the famous life-size, life-like marble statue surrounded by an orchidaceous Victorian iron fence in the Rotunda.

Governor John Garland Pollard said the statue had been appraised at $5 million but it might as well have been $50 million or $500 million. One does not sell one's ancestors, especially Father Washington.

Two buttons are missing from one side of Washington's coat and one from another. A janitor used to attribute the missing buttons to Martha Washington's poor housekeeping, but Dr. Douglas S. Freeman said it was the General's old military coat. Washington persuaded Jefferson to let him wear it for sculptor Jean Houdon rather than the fashionable toga.

Washington was in his prime, about 53, not long after the Revolutionary War. He became President at 57, so he was at ease between two crushing responsibilities. Yet the sculptor wrought two weeks to put the gravity in his brow.

One day as Houdon was working a fellow came to Mount Vernon to sell some mules. When the horse-trader mentioned the price, Washington's mouth tightened, and Houdon had him.

The grim-mouthed look and the attitude of force in his stance is his horse-trading posture. It's altogether fitting, right there between the two chambers of the Virginia General Assembly, where today's legislators

pause to talk and horse-trade, leaning on the orchid iron fence beneath Washington's severe and steady stare.

Washington came to approve the statue. He stood before it a moment, then went over into a corner, looked at it from there, nodded, and said he liked it. When the hostess tells tourists that, they say Ah-h-h-h, and go stand where Washington stood.

Virginia didn't dedicate the statue right away. Why rush? It was there, wasn't it? And not likely to go off. In due course, 134 years later, Governor Pollard collected a distinguished company, including a hallful of Washington descendants, and did the job in fine style, as everyone knew would be the case, one day.

At the ceremonies, the forward-looking John Stewart Bryan looked back long enough to recall an earlier proposal by *The Richmond News Leader* that the eight niches, "set apart with almost prophetic foresight" around the Rotunda in 1785, be filled with presentments of Virginia's other seven Presidents and that under the eighth, vacant space there be inscribed two words: *Virginia waits.*

It was a lofty thought, the kind Virginians love, but as it turned out the eighth space was filled fully as splendidly with the Houdon bust of Lafayette. Washington gazes directly into the eyes of his old friend and the godfather of our country.

Scarcely a week passes during an Assembly session but what some member doesn't arise to remind his colleagues that they are "members of the oldest living legislative body in continuous existence in the Western Hemisphere." It gives ever so much import to the opening and closing of

33

the squirrel season west of the Blue Ridge.

And there is, indubitably, a sense of continuity. Once when the phone rang in the office off the floor of the State Senate, Senate Clerk Ben Lacy picked it up, and a little old lady's voice quavered: "How are things going up there in the House of Burgesses?"

It all betokens the Commonwealth's comfortable co-existence with calendar, and clock.

Time waits for no one, a popular song suggests, but it waits for Virginians. They have grasped the unendingness of time, looking at it equally from either direction as if gazing up or down a river.

No stiff, Yankee-like partitions—so much gross wallboard—rear in their minds between yesterday, today, and tomorrow. All flow into one, and could just as easily be tomorrow, today, and, yesterday, and often are, in conversation.

In Virginia, the people, not the watches, *keep* time.

That limp watch, folded over a table edge in Salvador Dali's painting, is a Virginia watch, all wore out from trying to serve a people for whom time doesn't exist, except in eons, great oceans of eternity, in which they work, and bathe, and play, languorously.

When they speak of a long-gone relative or friend, or an ancestor a couple of jumps back, the laughter of love is in their eyes and a catch of excitement in their throats, as if he or she had just now stepped from the room and would be back; is back, in fact, with them.

An immensely able and persuasive Virginian, the tsar of his society, was speaking to me of his beloved Commonwealth, and in the fervor of establishing a point, he remarked, from his inmost being, and without conceit: "I have lived in Virginia 300 years."

He hesitated, in some awe, I thought, at his own audacity, but only to add: "On both sides of my family."

James Joyce's great short story, "The Dead," might have unfolded in Virginia instead of Dublin. A profound sense of the past grips a young man during the course of an evening in which he presides over a family Christmas dinner at his aunts', rides around a statue of a lost hero in the snow going home, and listens to his wife reminiscing about a vital young admirer who died romantically to impress her. The living and the dead commingle in the husband's mind as he drifts into sleep, and he rather thinks he is more dead than alive, measured against the idealist aflame in

34

his wife's memories.

Ordinarily, the story is viewed as an anatomy of a moribund community, but a Virginian would have had none of the young man's feelings of unworthiness, no sense of being a shade.

The past matters.

And without any apologies.

After all, that milieu produced Joyce, and he reproduced it.

And Virginians use the past much as does the artist, enjoying a kind of double life in the living and the telling, shaping it to their ends, finding rich meaning and color in the clay of existence.

They would regard the loss of memory by a community with much the same horror that they view amnesia in an individual.

There is a reassuring continuity in knowing that as they remember, they will be remembered.

The uses of the past, like those of adversity, are sweet, and they can be comrades-in-arms.

When Governor Pollard went about during the Depression placing statues in niches and digging in his own pockets for private, fund-raising dinners at the Mansion to found the Virginia Museum of Fine Arts, he was bent on more than mere beautification.

He understood, as only a former teacher could, the necessity of education, and he had counted on doing for schools what Governor Byrd had done for roads, but his hopes crashed with the stock market in 1929.

In raising statues to the great, he was rallying Virginians, recalling us to ourselves, saying: they did it, we can do it.

(Among the gallery of Governors in the State Capitol, his portrait is impish, an infectiously merry man, eyes beaming, asking, "Well, what now?", hands shoved in his pocket so that his open coat is pulled away from his paunch. "I got that," he used to say, patting his paunch, "from swallowing the Organization.")

Virginians want to teach their offspring the past, not so much for the glory of it, as to hand down certain qualities that have served well. The same man who had lived 300 years in Virginia would not stand being five minutes, or even a minute, late to an appointment.

They are conscious, intensely, of time as life.

THE HONEY IN THE HORSE

To many Virginians the past comes home most keenly through the yew-lined avenues of the Civil War. As children they refought the war in back alleys and front yards, when the most daring thing a boy could say was that he—or she, if a tomboy—would be Ulysses Grant, and on rainy days with toy soldiers on the floor, converting the patterns in the rug into concealing forests, protective rivers, and contested knolls. But with slightly different results—Stonewall survived, one-armed, at Chancellorsville; Jeb recovered at Yellow Tavern; Pickett's charge won Gettysburg, and Lee drove past Appomattox to join Johnston south of Danville, where the two turned and thrashed Grant and Sherman. Lee gallantly let Grant keep his sword. (There the curtain fell. The rain had ended, and, anyway, who could imagine a South alien from the nation?) At one period of childhood it was unbearable to read of the real war because it didn't coincide with the rug war.

But there's no escaping what Bruce Catton called the *Hamlet* of America. Even now you come in the deep wood upon a high, unexpected hill, rising suddenly brown with pine needles, and climb its steep, slippery sides and look down into the bowl of a great fortification time has captured with trees thicker in the trunk than a man's waist, and the trenches wind away from the fort and out of sight, convulsing the landscape, as if a massive mole had been that way, burrowing, and where once there was so much energy and desperate effort, there is silence.

36

And walking across a plowed field you stoop for a Miniè ball, and as you straighten, with the gray misshapen pellet in your fingers, it is as if a ragged yell had just died along a far fence row, with only a moment's lull in the rattle of musketry, and you almost see, and smell, the blue, drifting, acrid smoke where men fought, and nearly catch the echo, just that second past, of growling cannon behind the hill where cows graze. It is all there, only a leaf, a blade of grass, a second beyond our grasp, and it is as gone as if it had never been.

But the war keeps coming back in unexpected ways. A Richmond girl, now grown, used to direct a new date to her home on Monument Avenue by telling him that the tail of Jeb Stuart's horse pointed directly at her house.

Only recently the Nestor of Norfolk, a bold, free-wheeling thinker on whom people rely for a sense of the future, was talking with me, and, for the first time in many excited symposiums, the Civil War carromed into the conversation at some mention of Seven Pines. Suddenly my ardently progressive friend was in the saddle and riding into history, describing the battle down to the names of creeks, more knowledgeably than the men who fought there and knew it only as a friendly tree or a hateful rise of ground. At Seven Pines, he noted, Joe Johnston was wounded, and surely that was the most expensive shot in the war because Lee replaced him. (Catton, outlining the four big *ifs,* said that the first and biggest was that if Johnston had gone unhit at Seven Pines, the war might have ended that summer. Lee, he estimated, prolonged the conflict nearly three years.)

At the close of his gallop across the pastures of the past, my friend said, lightly, "But it was well they won."

And I, hastily and heavily, agreed, "Of course."

Even when the South was fighting, it had that in its heart, and Virginia more than any State because her sons had founded the nation, and Lee more than any soldier because he had modeled himself on Washington.

When the Army of Northern Virginia was marching on Sharpsburg, 20,000 men drifted away, primarily because they had joined to defend their homes, not invade the nation; and somebody remarked that this was no way to run an army, and Lee said, mildly, that it was no army, just an association of gentlemen trying to wage a war.

One camp was trying to save the States and the other struggling to hold together the Union and the two objectives need not have been mutually exclusive, and were, tragically, because at the very juncture that America was cursed with politicians of mediocre mind and motive, she produced military men of genius and nobility, and 600,000 died.

It is an instance, literally, in which if the military men had been in Congress, the war would never have begun, and if the politicians had been in the field, it would have collapsed.

In a crowning, crippling irony, the nation was deprived of Abraham Lincoln who could have eased, and speeded, a century's reconstruction.

Why does Virginia remember?

William Golding, the British novelist visiting Virginia as a teacher at Hollins College, suggested an answer in an essay, "Fable," published in a collection entitled *The Hot Gates*.

Golding wrote a fine novel, *Lord of the Flies,* which depicted a band of English boys plane-wrecked on a tropic island, and showed how their attempt to build a civilization "breaks down in blood and terror because the boys are suffering from the terrible disease of being human." His warning was that what happened in Germany could happen any place, even among the most innocent.

In his essay, he discovers the roots of the disease in prejudices handed down from generation to generation, "off-campus history" as opposed to a reasoned, objective study of our past and present selves.

Golding relates how a scholarly guide, taking him on a tour of Lee's retreat from Richmond, drove at a discreet 40 miles an hour, lecturing in a judicious, impartial tone, until they came to Appomattox, and his guide grunted, "Aw, shucks!" and drove past the place where Lee surrendered to Grant at 75 miles an hour.

"This is a different force from campus history. It is history felt in the blood and bones," wrote Golding. "Sometimes it is dignified by a pretty name, but I am not sure in my own mind that it is ever anything but pernicious. However, this is a political and historical question which we need not settle here and now."

Here and now, I think, is as good a place as any.

Golding's thesis about the dead past has merit, but what makes me suspect a broad application is the specific instance in which he chose to apply it.

I know Golding's guide who admires Lee. Indeed, leaving his home once, I noticed an engraving of Lee above his bookcase, and to tease my friend (and the mind of my son), I squared the boy toward the picture and said, "There's a man who mistook love for duty."

My friend said nothing.

He said very little to me for a solid week.

But he would have been as aggrieved at a slapdash assessment of a contemporary figure. One of the most civilized of beings, his blood-and-bone feeling for the past does not warp his judgment for the present or subdue his concern for the future. (Indeed, he arranged Golding's stimulating presence at Hollins.)

Lee was all that the South had left after the war.

(At little Washington College in Lexington, the trustees borrowed both the money and the new suit with which to send their rector to offer Lee the presidency.)

Without Lee the Lost Cause truly would be lost.

As a ghastly mistake, the war had little to commend it. It was blighted for the South by the issue of slavery, although few who fought had slaves.

What remained was the courage of thousands of brave men, whom Lee epitomized, and his own stately example in turning after the war to education, as clear a directive as the South ever received, and his refusal to complain. He led his people magnificently in moments of triumph, but he was greater in showing them how to dwell undefeated in defeat.

Scribbled on a paper found after his death were these words: "The gentleman does not needlessly and unnecessarily remind an offender of a wrong he may have committed against him. He cannot only forgive, he can forget. He strives for that nobleness of self and mildness of character which impart sufficient strength to let the past be but the past."

To let the past be but the past.

But Virginians insist on remembering him as an expression of what was worthiest in their cause, their State, and themselves. Through him they came to terms with the past.

If that hackneyed cry — "The South will rise again!" — is said in anything more than fun or self-derision, if it is to promote mischief in baiting others, then it is not in the spirit of Robert E. Lee.

Nor is it enough for us to resist witless acts of inhumanity or mere bad taste. If the Virginian is to draw strength from the past, it must be more than self-solace; he must harness his inspiration to tasks of his day or Lee's reach is incomplete, his mission undone. The region that knew Washington, Jefferson, and Lee should not be content to stumble in the rearguard of the States in efforts for schools and hospitals. It is not simply that a rank of about 40th is shameful in the roll call of the Union, but that the neglect is reflected in the lives of Virginia's people, and, most particularly, her youth.

There was no revanchism in Lee. When the president of Washington College walked by the drill field on the neighboring campus at the Virginia

Military Institute during a parade, he deliberately walked out of step with the drum.

Nor was there anything revanchist in the career of Lee's biographer, Dr. Douglas Southall Freeman. Daily he saluted the figure on horseback on his way to work at *The Richmond News Leader* where he enlightened his readers on the day's hard issues, even as he restored the heroic past in his study during the afternoon and evening.

Shuttling between the past and the present, he wove a sizeable body of legendary matter about himself in the process of depicting Washington and Lee. A sign above his office clock proclaimed: "Time alone is irreplaceable. Waste it not!" I remember, although no one else does, the sign's saying that time was irreplacable, which conveyed, I thought, an even better sense of time's remorseless sweep. Dr. Freeman stayed the hand by recapturing the past and pushed it forward by urging Virginians to greet the present vigorously.

Even as Freeman moved in Richmond between the Civil War and contemporary events, Lenoir Chambers in Norfolk did a towering work on Stonewall Jackson while editing *The Virginian-Pilot*. His theme was that Virginia could not rest with being merely "the best in the South." His editorials explaining the self-defeating policy of closing schools to prevent desegregation earned the Pulitzer Prize.

The editors, dealing with the news by day and moulding history by night, represented Virginia's creative tension between past and present, delving into one to inform and guide the other.

The bronze object of Freeman's salute was shipped into Richmond, like great pieces of armor plate, in four boxes aboard two flatcars on May 2, 1890, and then shifted to wagons. On May 7, with bands playing, men, women, and children in a crowd of 10,000 took hold of ropes attached to the trucks and moved to the site for the monument on the western edge of the city. Bits of rope still link some families to that May day.

Virginians love words, but on the pedestal's vast expanse, fairly aching for eloquence, they placed one word: *Lee*.

The equestrian statue, riding above the tree tops on Monument Avenue, often is in the city's consciousness.

In the 1930's someone saw bees swarming in and out of Traveler's mouth, and an apiarist disclosed he had been watching them for 20 years buzzing into the open mouth of the horse with their cargoes of pollen and honey. What drew them there he couldn't say because it must have taxed the patience even of bees to start a hive on a smooth metal base and then build a thick insulating wall of wax and resin to shield their home from the intense heat absorbed by the metal from the summer suns.

A tide of traffic, moving east and west, swirls by the statue which looks to the south, and it is the first thing that Richmonders meet in the morning as they enter the heart of the city to work and the last sight by night as they gain the green precincts of Monument Avenue going home, and the great still bronze figure above the rushing metallic tide is a reminder of the nobility of Lee which was the honey in the brazen inferno of the war, and it is best we never forget.

For it was hard-won honey.

SALT IN THE SOUTHWEST YET

There is a dichotomy in Virginia, in the lay of the land and the map of the mind— Eastern and Western Virginia (or, as they call it out there, the Mountain Empire.) Southwest Virginia's two notably grand features are her mountains, and men and women to match them.

It's a thing to make you grin to see a Virginia mountaineer's bobbing stride, as if he got it from stepping from ridge to ridge, over whole valleys, and hear his long talk. His attitudes stretch, too. Southwest Virginia remembers Cumberland Gap, the jumping off place. There's still a frontier swing to the walk, and the thought in Southwest Virginia.

The shade of Daniel Boone lingers there. (Virginia was the home base from which he roamed the wilderness. When Boone was 90, roasting venison on a ramrod, an interviewer asked him if he ever got lost, having no compass, "No," Daniel said. "I can't say as ever I was lost, but once I was *bewildered* for three days.")

When author Sherwood Anderson wanted surcease from cities, he came to Marion and built a house of fieldstone and logs, with rough plaster walls, called "Ripshin," for the nearby mountain creek. If he left his mark on the land (his gravestone overlooking Marion, says, "Life, not death, is the great adventure"), then some of the Southwest's humor and easy ways crept into his writing.

The Southwest's brand is evident in the Barter Theatre founded by Bob Porterfield in the Depression. He brought 22 actors from Broadway to Abingdon, with the novel idea of taking produce at the box office instead of across the footlights. It brought out the ham in the spectators, too. A farmer drove his cow to the door, set to work to get a pail of "admission," then strode into the theater, leaving his wife, saying, "Let her draw her own 35 cents."

In those early days Porterfield could take one look at the receipts and tell exactly who was inside: this one always a cake, that one plum preserves.

The Virginia General Assembly was just awakening to the importance of tourists. Porterfield hauled a large, tightly-packed barracks bag into a hearing of the budget committee.

"Gentlemen," he cried, "before you can attract tourists, you've got to have something to advertise!"

With that he slung the barracks bag in a great arc that snowed thousands of newspaper clippings over the astonished lawmakers. As he drove home his message, he saw one legislator after another reaching down slyly to pick up clippings to see if they were really about Barter.

"Virginia," Porterfield pleaded, "isn't getting enough after-dark entertainment."

"Young man," boomed a Senator, "what do you mean by after-dark entertainment?"

"That, sir," shot back Porterfield, "is the kind of entertainment you can go home and talk about."

"Give that boy his money!" roared the Senator.

The City of Roanoke is the Empire's gateway as it was when it was Big Lick, a frontier outpost in the French and Indian War, and, before that, when there were no men to call it anything, only the animals coming for salt at the lick. There's a saltiness yet in the spirit of the place.

In 1881 two merging railroads were considering four cities for a terminal headquarters. J. C. Moomaw persuaded Big Lick's leaders to subscribe a bonus of $10,000, and then he galloped through the night to present the bait to the railroads' officials conferring next day in Lexington.

"Gentlemen," said the Chairman, "this brings the road to Big Lick. This progressive spirit cannot be denied!"

Big Lick became Roanoke and took a slogan: "Acorn to Oak—Roanoke!" But now and then the residents refer to it by the old name, a salty reminder of the Magic City's buckskin beginnings.

To match Moomaw's famous ride to catch the trains, they tell of an earlier dash to get away from one, when the first train came steaming to Big Lick in 1852. An excited citizen, who had never seen a train, panicked and ran down the ties in front of the locomotive until the cowcatcher bumped him off the tracks.

Why, asked his friends, hadn't he climbed the banks?

"If I couldn't outrun it on the level," he panted, "what chance would I have uphill?"

No less quixotic were the races of horse-drawn fire companies in the 1890's. The contending chariots, thundering through the streets to the cheers of crowds, tried now and again to knock their rivals out of the running, a la Ben Hur, and, arriving at the fire, trained their hoses on each other, while the barn burned. Things are tamer now.

But occasionally the old spirit flares in a town where men ran on foot against trains and fire fighters fought each other in grand disdain of the fire. When Vice-President Nixon toured Roanoke in the 1956 campaign, the City scented the main street in pine oil—a case of execrable timing, cried a Democrat. "They should have waited until after Nixon left," he said.

Whence arises this happy dissent?

Somewhat in the geography.

When even an ordinary mortal steps off the plane onto the flat table-land hemmed by blue mountains, a cup held high in the hills, he feels an urge to shout and cavort across the bold landscape.

And more than somewhat in the people.

Big Lick lay on the Great Road to the Wilderness. Those that stopped off included Scotch Presbyterians, who opposed slavery on principle, and strong-minded German, Dutch, and Swiss individualists. Royal Governors welcomed them as a buffer between Tidewater and the Indians.

They brought their belongings on their backs, or on a packsaddle shaped from the forked branch of a tree. (*A History of Roanoke*, compiled by the WPA, relates that a pioneer preacher broke off in mid-sermon to declare: "Yonder is one of the best forks for a packsaddle I ever saw in these woods, and when services are over we will get it.")

Railroads fed newcomers into the population during the first half of the 20th century, and after World War II Northerners and Mid-westerners flocked into Roanoke at a rate to rank with the colonial migrations. The pioneer tradition persists, sometimes at odds with the temper of the rest of the State.

But if there's an East and West in Virginia, they meet, and the State is the stronger for the tension and the interplay. In 1963 the General Assembly visited Tidewater to see the newly-opened Chesapeake Bay Bridge-Tunnel, a striding Gulliver that at points has its footing 100 feet beneath the ocean's surface and at other times soars 75 feet above it.

A Senator from the Southwest noticed that the bridge-tunnel islands were buttressed by boulders, big as cars, hauled from his native hills, and later at Norfolk he saw a long freight train loaded with coal from Wise County. "We're in this thing together," he said.

THE MANY VIRGINIAS

Roanoke's early reliance on the railroads is matched by Norfolk's alliance with the Navy. If the Navy left, some observers used to say, Norfolk would sink.

But no more.

If the ships sailed away, Norfolk would weather that blow in some spectacular way which would win another award as an All-American City.

Nature gave Norfolk a supreme port, but the city's emergence waited on her own energies. Virginia's thinking, as Jean Gottmann noted, has been continental, shaped, as with the profile of the State itself, like a nicked Indian spearhead pointing into the interior of America. Virginia turned her back to the sea as the settlers pushed into the boundless frontier of that other ocean, the Wilderness.

Norfolk's phoenix-rise from Depression's ashes began in 1938 when 350 persons met in a junior high school to debate whether to abandon the Community Chest, which had failed 13 out of 15 years.

They would try once more, they decided, a referendum on Norfolk's future.

The drive carried that year, and has ever since. It serves to keep the city alert to its needs and also as a kind of test for young men entering public life, who start at the bottom rung of the United Givers Fund, much as Indian youths used to whip themselves with willow branches and starve in the desert.

In 1946 the community leaders carried their crusade into the City Council race, and won, and, more significantly, never lost touch. In 1949 Council appropriated $25,000 to study slums, and Norfolk was ready to become the first city to execute a loan and grant under the Housing Act of 1949. Norfolk became a model of urban renewal.

(And Norfolk heard one of the first voices to offer a way to restore the dwindling powers of the States. Former Governor Darden urged in April, 1963, that they be given the responsibility of directing Federal grant programs, such as urban renewal.)

Norfolk's makeup is a blend of N's—Navy, NATO, natives, and newcomers, especially North Carolinians—but it operates largely on nerve. A handful, or even a loner, will launch an idea, while others watch, smiling, the quixotic quest, and if it succeeds, as it generally does, smile at themselves for having smiled at its chances.

Somewhere in Norfolk it is always High Noon.

Everybody wanted "quality education," and so the Norfolk City Council proposed a sales tax, which everybody opposed as ruining the economy, but pig-headed Council persisted in defiance even of those who had pioneered other changes, and soon all Virginia cities were adopting the tax, like boys at follow-the-leader, until, finally, even the timorous General Assembly tumbled into it in 1966.

Some of this breeziness is due to the port, which soothes, as well as excites. A businessman, beset by a vexing telephone call, was maintaining his calm at some cost to his nervous system, his eyes fixed unseeingly on a clock set at an angle in a five-story tower outside his office window, when, suddenly, seemingly out of the face of the clock itself, crept the great, gray profile of an aircraft carrier, a moving portion of the city's skyline, and, watching, mesmerized, the carrier's slow, stately passage between the buildings, a miracle that time had produced, he relaxed. "I just saw a carrier go by," he told his excited caller quietly. "Look out your window."

Amid the dynamism, Norfolk keeps a solid clutch on the past, like a person leaving home in a hurry, grabbing what's most dear. This regard was manifest in the crusades of Mrs. Frantz Naylor to fix in public memory the landing of the first settlers at Cape Henry.

But it was only one of many which engaged her energies, including the providing of school lunches for underprivileged children, a pioneering concept that spread across America.

(Virginia women have been the driving force, the troops, in nearly every humanitarian advance in the Old Dominion, starting in this century with the great May campaign of 1905 to upgrade public schools into something resembling a system. The Virginia seal depicts an amazon with her foot on the head of a tyrant. More appropriately, it should show a member of the League of Woman Voters or the Virginia Federation of Women's Clubs presenting a petition to a legislator.)

It is a city of shopping centers, one merging into another, sometimes so vast that when thoroughfares intersect the motorist knows the eerie sensation of knowing no street boundaries, simply cruising an unlimited asphalt bay, in which he could just as easily be going any one of four ways.

Some find the scene sterile, but riding through the jumping, jittery neon night by bold, flamboyant signs of weird off-color colors of red, green, and orange is like driving through a three-dimensional Stuart Davis painting. I am not of that school of thought which finds everything in nature inspiring except man. Even en masse he is vital.

Covering acres is an open air market which offers, under one cope, a pizza parlor, with three handlers turning out an assembly line of pies to a waiting line of addicts; a florist shop full of simpering cement satyrs, as well as flowers, real and artificial; a super market with schools of fish on banks of ice and great-wheeled wagons loaded with melons; a steakhouse with steers turning on twin spits; an automatic laundry; a bakery with 23 kinds of doughnuts; a delicatessen with three kinds of submarines; a wine cellar, a toy department, and an airport. With jet runways.

If these prospects displease, there is, for Il Penseroso, not far away, the ride across Lynnhaven Bridge, and a view across the vast, calm Bay dotted almost to its center with men, women and children, like water spiders on a pond, a sight to delight Breughel.

And a little further, Seashore State Park, with huge silent dunes, stretching and yawning in the hot sand sun, and secret creeks, and lagoons of black water in which gaunt cypress trees, draped in gray moss, stand, and reflect, time's sentinels, and the main trails, like wide aisles in the Forest of Fontainebleau, along which trip tourists clad in shorts.

And smack in the City of Chesapeake, the greatest metropolis in land area in the United States, the Dismal Swamp, once large as a state, now being nibbled away, but please save a shaggy portion to sustain us in megalopolis with the thought that, though we won't, we could, if we would, get lost in its depths, at least in the dim recesses of the imagination.

Across the river from Norfolk is Portsmouth, and the two gaze, now and then, amazed over the water at each other's changing skyline, like growing youths who have been separated for a summer. In the heart of Portsmouth is Old Portsmouth, unlike other town-house sections of Virginia in that it never sank into blight but just went living quietly in old lace until the young ones began to come back and spruce it up, but there was, really, very little to do. There is a double richness in sons' returning to the neighborhood of their fathers, a coming back and a carrying forward.

The Northern Neck specialized in producing Presidents of the United States (three of them—Washington and Monroe from Westmoreland County and Madison from adjoining King George, plus Robert E. Lee, a Westmoreland man) and is still a breeding ground of gentlemen and gentle men, among them two former members of the Virginia House of Delegates, W. Tayloe Murphy and R. Hill Fleet.

One primary election the two campaigned for the same House seat. Fleet didn't have a car, so Murphy invited him to share his, and the two adversaries drove together all around Northern Neck.

When they reached a farm, Murphy would go up and talk to the family, and then he'd come back to the car while Fleet took his turn with the voters. Between stops they talked about how the campaign was going and what a trial it was to have to go through although, as they observed, they had the pleasure of each other's company.

At one house after Murphy returned to the car, Fleet joined the farmer and made a stirring plea.

"You talk fine, Mr. Murphy," said the farmer, "but that fellow in here ahead of you, Hill Fleet, impressed me so much I'll have to vote for him."

"Don't feel a bit bad about it," said Fleet firmly. "That gentlemen who preceded me is the salt of the earth."

So they were, both of them, as are all natives of Northern Neck.

The saying on the Neck is " 'deed I do!" and " 'deed I don't" and " 'deed it is!" and " 'deed I won't!", thick as whippoorwill cries through their speech, and 'deed I do pray it never dies. A recent traffic sign in Kilmarnock set the pace in Northern Neck. It said: "Please don't double-park long." The natives speak of the newcomers as "com' 'eres."

Across from the Neck is the Eastern Shore, made up of the two neighboring counties of Northampton and Accomack hung out across the bay from the main body of Virginia like a stocking that Santa Claus forgot.

Just off Eastern Shore is the island of Assateague from which wild ponies are herded annually to the island of Chincoteague for auctioning by the local firemen who play tidal cowboy once a year.

All is well at the roundup until time to separate the foals from their dams, and then the mares bawl, the colts whinney, and the women tourists lean against their cars and weep, and it is no place for a strong man. Everybody is misty.

If some of the ponies leave their haven, few of the people do, and many of those who remain are kin. Indeed, their customary remark on meeting family groups from the mainland is: "I see the favor!"

Some maps of the Old Dominion omit the Eastern Shore, but such an exclusion would isolate the rest of the State from felicity because, more than a stocking left on the line, the Shore is a cornucopia which produces nearly 70 per cent of the truck farm produce consumed in Virginia. Completion of the Chesapeake Bay Bridge-Tunnel was supposed to bring the Shore a bonanza; and some residents, braced for the full-blown benefits of the 20th Century, did not know whether to be glad or sad when a boom did not arrive in one jump with the cutting of the Bridge-Tunnel ribbon. It's a little like waiting for Godot.

And across the harbor from Portsmouth and Norfolk is Newport News, saved once by news of Captain Newport's bringing provisions to the settlers, but never lifted much beyond the obscurity of a rural postoffice until another bearer of good tidings, Collis P. Huntington, brought a railroad and built a shipyard in 1889.

When his plan for a single transcontinental railway system fell apart, Huntington was left with the Chesapeake and Ohio, with its eastern terminus at Newport News fronting on a splendid deep water harbor. He decided to establish a shipyard "right at the gateway to the sea" where

"there is never any ice in winter, and it is never so cold but you can hammer metal out of doors."

Huntington underwrote the heavy losses on the first contracts, and out of his orders, the Yard forged the motto:

WE SHALL BUILD GOOD SHIPS HERE
AT A PROFIT — IF WE CAN
AT A LOSS — IF WE MUST
BUT ALWAYS GOOD SHIPS

It is a little difficult to fix the flexing boundaries of Newport News because at any moment a part of her may be off China or under the North Pole.

A sizeable chunk is the USS Enterprise. The nuclear carrier is simply the biggest ship in the world as a thousand statistics testify (the weight, 86,000 tons, doubles that of the biggest battleships), but no figure can convey the look of her, a gray, towering headland, at the end of a line of ships at the Norfolk Naval Base. (There is, or ought to be, a natural symbiosis between Newport News, which births, and Norfolk, which berths the ships.) You wonder, at the first glimpse of the great, gray, clean-edged

mass if she can really be that big. Her sheer size, rising in a great arc, reminds you more of the excesses of nature—a moving wall of rain—than anything man-made.

She keeps getting bigger, until standing alongside her (29 stories high from keel to mast) is like being involved in a giant feature of the landscape, an overwhelming cliff, with a great indent in its side, or an immense plateau in the Grand Canyon.

She's faster than the swiftest liner, more than 40 miles an hour without flagging, as she sweeps along, a huge hand, palm up, for her birds, the 100 planes she carries.

Its streaming length is like a lance at sea.

Newport News also launched William Styron, a major American novelist, whose frigates will be bearing rich freight long after the Enterprise is scrap.

Among such prestigious installations as NASA and Langley Field, Hampton has two junior high schools named for Thomas Eaton and Benjamin Syms, colonists who in 1634 set up the nation's first school fund with a farm, two milch cows, and some money, from which Hampton's schools still realize, annually, $200 which goes into teacher scholarships. Hampton is also the spot where in the winter of 1607 the Kecoughtan Indians fed broiled oysters to John Smith who remarked that never did he eat so well. They are still good.

And up the river is Richmond, seated, like Rome, a serene Queen on seven hills, though few can agree on which seven, and where, like Rome, all roads lead, with two great department stores, twin arms of a magnet drawing customers from as far away as North Carolina, and Capitol Square, erupting in greenery, and biennial oratory.

The vignette most often deemed emblematic of Richmond is a strikingly beautiful *grande dame* pedaling a bicycle determinedly ·through churchgoing traffic along downtown Franklin Street, a dachshund running by the rear wheel, as if caged, squirrel-like, in its spokes. Startled visitors have exclaimed: "There goes Richmond!"

They compliment the city. Elizabeth Bocock is among its most progressive spirits—tall, queenly as the first Elizabeth, with a vivacity of mind to match her eager face, necessarily strong to frame the direct, brown eyes.

The church to which she pedals is St. Paul's, where the great bell in the tower strikes with a heavy swish, as through dense rushes, as if time is thicker there, and the chimes ripple slowly across Capitol Square. Arriving at a congregational business meeting, Mrs. Bocock asked her companion, "What is that model up there?"

Her friend, Mrs. Carl Fleming, said it was a proposed addition to the parish house, to be built in an L around the neighboring business college.

"I never saw such lack of foresight," said Mrs. Bocock.

She provided for the purchase of the full site, and, in such fashion, acts as Richmond's fairy godmother, restoring old homes, turning over most of her own stone mansion to the Senior Center and then to the Richmond Professional Institute for domitory space. "It pleases me," said Mrs. Fleming, "to think of Elizabeth in the midst of that RPI explosion." It is, indeed, pleasing to think of students, who deplore all conformity but their own, presented with the edifying sight of the lovely iconoclast preserving the best of the past for the future.

Beyond Richmond is Northern Virginia which, until recently, some Virginians considered beyond Virginia. Opposing a bill to permit Federal employes to hold public office, a legislator suggested in 1954 that Arlington was populated largely with the nation's crackpots. Later, he amended it to say it only contained those that had not gone to Los Angeles and Hollywood.

Some members suspected *any* urban area and agreed with State Senator Charles T. Moses of Appomattox who said, quite frankly, that the reins of government ought to rest in the hands of those who turned the sod and fed the hogs.

When some of his colleagues were skirting an issue, the man from Appomattox would arise and lay it open beyond any mincing mending. He saw his senatorial colleagues who disagreed with him as only temporary foes but abiding friends. Once when Senator Moses had lost a round, he stopped at the desk of William B. Spong Jr. of Portsmouth, dropped a hand on the younger man's shoulder, and said: "Billy, ain't you *EVER* gonna vote with me on *ANYTHING.*"

By 1966, under the impact of court-ordered reapportionment, one of the fairest in the land, the Virginia General Assembly's city and county boys were voting together on many things, a harmony embracing even Northern Virginia. At the rate of its growth, Northern Virginia might soon embrace the rest of the state, anyway. (The population of Prince William County jumps 50 per cent every 10 years.)

Life seems intenser there. A candidate for State-wide office reported being approached by two women with the same question but opposite views, who fell to arguing with each other so vehemently that he drifted away without answering either.

Speculation used to be how Northern Virginia, with more than 70 per cent of its population non-native, could become one with the rest of Virginia. But with lead-time in solving problems of mass transportation, water and air pollution, and traffic patterns, Northern Virginia can guide and help ease the transition for the remainder of the Old Dominion. Paradoxically, the journey may be smoother, with less jolts to old ways, because the crackpots banged along the trail first.

Virginians used to speak of the Old Dominion with a sigh, fond or frustrate, as if it were unvarying—one Virginia—but, increasingly, they see many Virginias, each capable of contributing wisdom to the others, even, astonishingly, Northern Virginia, next door to Washington.

But there is tradition for this, too. You never escape the past in Virginia.

Madison and Jefferson bargained with Hamilton to have the Capitol placed on the Potomac where Virginia could keep an eye on her daughter, the nation.

Old Virginia, new Virginia, same Virginia.

WHY THEY STAY

One comforting thing about Virginians is their quiet acceptance of their own merit. None of this toeing the ground and saying, Oh, I'm really not all that good. With Gilbert and Sullivan's Wandering Minstrel, the Virginians sing: "We really know our worth, the Sun and I."

To commemorate the 350th anniversary of the landing at Jamestown, a company went back to England in 1957. Legend says that as a group was being presented to Queen Elizabeth, she murmured that they must feel cramped on the tiny island after so large a country as America.

"Why, your majesty," one of them reassured her, "it's no smaller than Virginia!"

Virginians' unflinching self-esteem must have prompted William Faulkner's reply when he was asked why he became a writer in residence at the University of Virginia.

"Because I like your country, Virginia and Virginians," he said. "Virginians are all snobs. I like snobs. A snob spends so much time being a snob he has none left to bother other people."

Virginians applauded.

The dark-eyed hunter from Mississippi roamed the Lawn for several years among the carefree, strolling youths, and on another occasion delivered another judgment.

Other Southern states, said Faulkner, are faintly ashamed when Virginia does something not in the best taste. They expect better of her, as does a child of its mother.

The shared sense of guilt must arise in part because Virginia is the Mother State, not only of Presidents (five of the first six, eight in all) but also of eight states from her original holdings (Kentucky, Ohio, Wisconsin, West Virginia, Indiana, Illinois, Michigan, and Minnesota), and whole populations of people who were born in Virginia and then scattered.

Virginia's role as a feeder of people to other regions was examined by John Melville Jennings, director of the Virginia Historical Society, in *Exploring Virginia's Human Resources.* The 1850 census found 388,000 persons in other states claiming the Old Dominion as their birthplace. Virginia at that time had 949,000 inhabitants.

In *Virginia:The English Heritage in America,* Parke Rouse Jr. notes that in a 150-year span beginning in 1774, "at least 329 men born within Virginia's present boundaries served other states as delegates to the Continental Congress, United States Senators, and Representatives in Congress." Among the emigres were Henry Clay of Hanover County, the Kentucky compromiser, and Stephen Austin of Wythe County and Sam Houston of Rockbridge County who went to Texas to help found an empire within an empire.

From waves of wandering FFV's (far flung Virginians, a city editor of mine called them), succeeding generations have racial memories that stir when they come back to Virginia or meet a Virginian or read in the papers of an incident that doesn't square with their atavistic estimate of the Mother State.

Dr. Jean Gottmann, author of *Virginia at Mid-Century,* commented on high densities of population in Southwest Virginia over a variety of sections. "As a result of the some psychological attitude," he wrote, "the local people remain within this area whether or not the economic conditions make it reasonable and attractive to do so."

These descend from the bide-a-whiles who bade Daniel Boone goodbye when he struck out through the Cumberland Gap. They have counterparts in Roanoke, Richmond, and Norfolk who turn down a promotion because it entails a transfer to another state; or, if they go, they leave determined to come back, some day. And often do.

In plain language, they love it.

They have the feeling they would not be themselves, deprived of looking now and then at a dogwood curtseying whitely amid tall pines.

They'd be lacking, they fear, if once in a while they couldn't set their feet on the amiable, uneven surface of a sidewalk of herringbone brick.

Or lean on an iron fence of short, black, hand-pikes guarding a magnolia tree dark-glistening in the sun, wadded white blossoms scattered about its folds like a careless Southern belle airily strewing handkerchiefs and gloves wherever she goes.

They'd be lost without the brave sight of hollyhocks nodding tall, gay, high-piled heads beside a gray, weatherbeaten shack, gregarious flowers which will grow anywhere, in well-tended beds, or in a straggling, laughing troupe along a dusty roadside.

Without certain restorative odors, they'd be pale and wan.

Former Governor Colgate W. Darden Jr., after he turned down a seat in the United States Senate and took the presidency of the University of Virginia, was conscious of some ingredient left out of that intellectual ferment. He couldn't put his finger on it. Wasn't he undertaking successfully his own dream, to realize Jefferson's long-deferred dream of a great capstone in Charlottesville for public education? Then, traveling to Norfolk one Saturday, he caught, just outside of Petersburg, a tonic whiff of salt sea breeze, and knew, a Tidewater boy nearing home, what had been missing.

Commonwealth Editor Jim Wamsley, revisiting a coal camp in Southwest Virginia after 20 years, smelled the fumes from burning slag at a drift mouth mingling, fighting with the clean, pine-swept mountain air; and, as he got out of the car and stood snuffing, it was as if he had just left, the sulphurous odor recapturing the past as poignantly as the madeleine Marcel dipped in tea.

An exile from Danville hurrying along Main Street in Richmond sniffs the sudden, rich, tawny fragrance of Tobacco Row factories and remembers the golden hands hanging in his father's Southside tobacco barn, along with his family's hopes, when a year's crop hinged on a minute's spiel by an auctioneer. He breaths deeply of the past.

And then there are foods that smell and taste, of home to the Virginian.

The main thing to know about William Byrd II's "Secret Diary" is that nearly every entry begins and ends with what he ate.

When Dolly Madison, who grew up at "Scotchtown", was presiding at the White House, the wife of the British minister criticized her dinners as being like "harvest-home" suppers. That was the Virginian in Dolly.

She served, no doubt, sweet corn, so tender that the kernels practically melted with the butter, and tomatoes, from her home in Hanover, so large that a single slice almost filled the plate, and if there was country ham, then surely, somewhere within reach, a white porcelain boat of rich, brown, red-eye gravy, and if gravy, certainly grits, and, having spent her childhood in Virginia, she would have greens of some sort, collards, perhaps, which horrified the British minister's wife. You grow up only tolerating collards, and then one day, when you are far away from home, in California, or the White House, you miss them. And quite possibly there was Southern fried chicken, and somebody, who had been the youngest in a family of nine asked for the neck because, being the youngest, he acquired a taste for it that meant home to him thereafter and nobody eats the neck any more and what monotony to look around the table and see nothing but drumsticks, and how long has it been since two people leaned across the table to pull a wishbone as they did at Dolly's that night, to the consternation of the British minister's wife. On the side, perhaps, were home-preserved damsons, piquant and dark-purple, the seeds still in, along with butter, fresh-churned, pale as a new moon, with a wheat sheaf wood-stamped on it, and so lissome that you had to move quick transferring it from your knife to the biscuit, smoking hot. My mind keeps returning to that fried chicken, remembering how in a large Southern family everybody had a particular piece—Bob, the back; Neddy, the breast; Ida, the wing, and so on, with Momma, when she finally got to sit down, the gizzard, and this parceling of the chicken must have demoralized Mrs. Anthony Merry, the ambassador's wife, but presently, the dessert came, and, wonders, it was a watermelon, which, when cut, fell apart, ker-r-r-ack, as if a moiety of the world had split, as Shakespeare, or somebody, said, and there was a rosy glow playing above the two halves, and a smell as of new-morn, new-mown grass, and everyone said he or she had never seen a finer melon, which everyone always says, and it is true because none is finer than the one before you, and surely there was no finer table than Dolly Madison's.

It is not the mere eating, but the company, and the lingering long at the table that Virginians love, and the sense of having survived the week and come together again for nourishing the spirit for another go at life, but most of all it is simply that we are here, looking in each other's eyes and smiling and exclaiming over the food, and for the moment, at least, life is as tender as the sweet corn that practically melts with the butter.

The days would be dull, indeed, without a cardinal's steady, stropping whistle from a tulip tree in Bristol; the meditative phrases of a wood thrush —singing, listening, singing again—along a creek in the late afternoon in Goochland; the bobwhite's pert salute from a briar patch in King William, and the mourning doves' hailing the morning from a pine at Big Stone Gap, but mostly, and everywhere, and at all times, the mockingbird.

He perches on a chimney, and he is the last thing we hear at night, racketing away in the moonlight as if there was no tomorrow, a Villon of a bird, and the first thing in the morning, pouring out his song, an endless bounty; and at midday still singing while flying jerkily from tree to fence, as if tossed about by the music inside him.

He is Southern, too, in his sociability, always messing in somebody's business—diving, chiding, at a passing dog; demanding at the backdoor that someone bring raisins; fighting his reflection in the window. There's no going through life without knowing the family next door for the mockingbird. He is as intense a part of the scene, as much into things, as children playing in a sandpile or housewives hanging out wash and calling from yard to yard. The mockingbird is with it, every minute, an inextricable feature of the day or night in Virginia.

When Betty Roane Priddy was a child in Ashland (and note that double first name, a Virginia custom), a mockingbird sat on the chimney and sang as she practiced at the piano, stopping when she paused, picking up when she began again, seeming to try to follow the very notes when she went over a passage several times. Which is why, no doubt, when you drive through Hanover County, you are apt to hear a mockingbird cut loose with something that sounds startlingly like "O'er the flow'ry spangled grass trips the lovely ama-ryl-lis." It is a remarkable bird.

A friend, an English scholar, finds the scent of the skunk interesting. He became aware of its nuances in driving around the Valley of Virginia as a newspaperman and would miss it now, he says.

The first deep waft of a skunk, he contends, is not unlike the aroma of strong, black coffee, heavy with chickory, and, as it begins to fade, the last, faint whiff has a hint of mint. I don't know.

But I can testify to the highly tactile world of Virginia: the first, steadying reassurance against the cheek of the applesmooth, walnut-hard stock of a shotgun; the exciting tug of a line as a bass hits a plug; the ornate heaviness of grandfathah's mothah's to-mah-to servah, a cool, cur-licued handle to a way of life through four or more generations; the feel of power of a horse beneath the leather; the sudden, light, lifting when he takes a jump, and the coming down, to find him still there, and, magically, the staying on. ("A Virginian," said Fitzhugh Lee, "teaches his sons to ride, shoot, and tell the truth.")

Virginians do not let go these things easily. When the board of super-visors sought to pave a dirt road in Fauquier, dozens of taxpayers turned out to protest in behalf of the horses' feet.

Returning from trips out of State, Senator Harry Byrd Sr. liked to play a little game by insisting he could feel the moment his car was passing into Virginia. It's just *different,* he said.

Some Virginians-in-exile harbor the secret notion, though they know it absurd, that no matter what gret thing they do, it isn't as sweet because it ain't taking place in the context of the friends and family for whom they care the most. It somehow don't count. What's the good of realizing your friends' fine expectations among strangers?

A generation or so back, mothers sometimes discouraged their daugh-ters from marrying otherwise highly acceptable suitors simply because they came from some far off, godforsaken spot like Baltimore. But where would you *live*? they wailed.

This love of place explains why Virginians, especially women, are fond of tracing relatives and discovering mutual friends and acquaintances as if their community was one large family that had to be accounted for in all its members before the conversation could turn, with a sigh, to other channels. It is not necessary that the persons have "been somebody" only that they have been there.

Sometimes, as two Virginia women converse, one will mention a person —say, Washington Moncure—and the other will say, "Oh, yes I know Washington Moncure!", and trace the family through all its branches, out to the very twigs and back to the roots, only to have the first one murmur, "I was talking about the *other* Washington Moncure!", and off they go again.

The mother of a teenager was remarking how upset she used to get as a girl at her own mother's automatic question when the daughter had a new caller: "Who is his father?"

"Oh, what difference does *that* make?" she cried, back in the 1930's, to her mother.

And then, she said, just the other day a boy invited her own teenage daughter to the high school junior prom, and, to the mother's chagrin, she heard herself asking: "Who is his father?"

"So I went over and apologized to my mother for being so impatient at her interest 30 years ago, and when I finished, my mother asked: 'Who *is* his father?'"

What mystifies visitors is that with all this interest in origins, a Virginian with distinguished forebears is as loath to disclose it as if they were Frank and Jesse James.

The wife of Bishop Beverley Tucker was one of the last of the Washington family to live in the white-pillared mansion overlooking the Potomac, but in a company discussing ancestries when someone asked about hers, she said, shyly, she was only a farm girl.

What farm? somebody wanted to know, after she had gone.

Mount Vernon, said somebody else.

This disposition to fill in the background is not confined to women. The men are as prone to talk, a tendency that causes an advertising friend

62

some difficulty with his New York headquarters. It's as if he's in a foreign land, trying to explain Virginia.

"New York doesn't understand that you don't start doing business directly with Virginians," he said. "You've got to win their attention, by talking about a dozen other things. Peavining, they call it, and don't ask me where the term started, except I understand pea vines run all over the place."

"Aren't you peavining now?" I asked.

"Maybe. It grows on you. Maybe Virginians fell into the habit because so many of them grow up together and went to the same school and played on the same team and sometimes courted the same girls, and now their children are having their teachers and go to the same cotillion, so there's not only the past to finger and touch lovingly, but even more wonderfully, the present to compare to it—so that they see a mother's eyes in her son's and a father's way of talking in a girl's speech—and the future to conjure, and alongside all that, business can wait a while. It's not hookworm, or anything," he added. "It's a way of life."

"Is it beginning to bother you?" I asked.

"It's beginning not to bother me," he said. "That's what bothers New York."

But working counter to this interest in origins is a natural friendliness that moves Virginians to welcome newcomers warmly and give them quickly a feeling of belonging, with the result that some nouveau Virginians are more perfervidly Virginian than the natives. So, in a way, to be a Virginian, you need only be there, or even, with General MacArthur, intend to have been there. It is best just not to think about it.

What Faulkner divined as a sense of decency in Virginians is manifest in the State government's insistence on honesty. A friend told me how he watched, in growing suspense, a television documentary indict state after state on a map of the Eastern Seaboard for corruption in highway construction. Finally, and to his relief, the only state that escaped the taint was Virginia.

Another friend, the purchasing department chief in a regional firm, described the disbelief, and then the approval, of out-of-state salesmen on learning that there is no "man to see" in Virginia government.

But honesty in fiscal affairs is not enough, as Governor Harrison once observed. There also must be honesty in appraising broad problems.

A DIVERSITY OF GOVERNORS

Something about a Virginia Governor sets him apart, Virginians like to think—a dignity, a courtliness, and, on most occasions, a refusal to be stampeded, or, indeed, at certain times to be moved at all. Among politicians, the Governor's chair is akin to the siege perilous at Camelot, and the office itself is the Grail a-glimmering through the trees. The least a man can do if he wins is behave.

Senator Harry Byrd Sr. spoke of his four years in the Mansion as the happiest of his career and called the Governor's chair the highest honor within the power of Virginia to bestow; and Governor Almond, who seldom let anybody top him oratorically, once added, "or, indeed, the world."

Senator Byrd, I sometimes suspected, sought to shammy the revolving cup (nobody can have the coveted office for successive terms) both to keep his contending lieutenants on their toes and divert their ambitious eyes from his own seat in the Senate.

And, indeed, it is a grand thing even to have *been* a Virginia Governor.

"The real thing that sets him apart is the people's confidence in the office," said a former Governor. "You just can't fail. They won't let you."

Tourists, hearing about "the Governor's Mansion," expect an edifice on the order of Mount Vernon and often pass the Mansion without even noticing the violet-gray structure, square as a child's block, set in the back corner of the Square. In its unobtrusive good taste, it is typically Virginian; and, also typically, Virginians enjoy watching you grow aware of its understated elegance.

The Mansion has an aura of memories: Governor Battle padding out barefoot at 4 A.M. to pull a stray dog out of the swan fountain . . . Governor Almond, called to the phone by the butler to talk to "a Mister Kimmerly," discovering he was in conversation with John F. Kennedy . . . newly-elected Governor Stanley, welcoming reporters to a budget briefing, causing them to flinch instinctively when, seeking to ease the tension with a story, he drew back his long arm at the punch line as if to throw a rock . . . Governor Byrd's guest, Winston Churchill, strolling downstairs and handing a formally dressed Richmonder a quarter to go fetch him a paper . . . Forthright Governor Tuck, deciding one night to run a security test in the Square. Stepping out in the yard, he fired a pistol in the air and held his watch to see how long it would take the Capitol police to reach him. "And not only that," he told Governor Darden later, "I blew my whistle. When they finally got here, their knees were knocking so, they scared me. That police force you left me isn't worth a damn!"

A ghostly lady roams the Mansion, according to legend. I don't believe it. There's no room. For they are all there, together, in the Square, a diversity of Governors.

Among the Governors since Byrd, rangy, quiet George C. Peery established the Alcoholic Beverage Control system, demanded a minimum eight months' school term, put a tax on utilities for public schools in the tail end of the Depression, and, when he got ready to go back to Tazewell, pointed in his office and said, "That chair there is the one thing you can take home with you from Richmond."

One anti-Organization candidate, James H. Price, gained the Governor's chair, and, to show he had been there, left sound budget procedures, some of them being adopted only now, and a great building in the shape of a cross, the Medical College of Virginia Hospital, which he obtained through Federal funds.

Of those I covered, there is Colgate W. Darden Jr., the most philosophical. Anywhere he appears, reporters flock around him excitedly, soaring and gliding in the powerful updrafts and dizzying drops of his conversation.

Among many achievements—a probation and parole setup, the personnel act, the retirement system—Virginians cherish most Darden's abiding interest in education, which, after all, is the main thing. He struck with all his strength, in and out of office, wherever he saw an opening

Byrd   *Pollard*   *Peery*

for that cause. (Summoned to a hastily collected conference of State college presidents on subsidized athletics in 1955, he improved the occasion—and shook the Organization—by demanding "categorical assurances" from the State's leadership that no child would be denied an education during the desegregation upheaval.)

To Virginians, he is a patient Pericles, responding (without a single I-told-you-so) when requested to guide the reopening of public schools in Prince Edward County, striving on the State Board of Education to extend quality schooling everywhere. He waged a one-man crusade for education.

During the strike-ridden era after World War II, when the rest of the nation was turbulent, Virginia was, as the author of the stability put it, "as cool as the center seed of a cucumber." William Munford Tuck so filled the stage with his actions and reactions that the people of the State sat enthralled. It was like watching Shakespeare—Caesar bestriding the world, or, better still, an entire troupe performing Henry IV, Part I. He dominated the scene, and Virginia became a spectator State.

When employes of the Virginia Electric and Power Company threatened to walk out after a labor disagreement, Governor Tuck dusted off a statute of 1785, and threatened to enlist them in the militia of Virginia, which existed mostly in the Governor's mind.

66

Price   *Darden*   *Tuck*

His Attorney General had advised the Governor that he lacked the power to interfere, but the Governor told the Attorney-General to find the authority, or the Governor would find another Attorney-General. That the Attorney-General was an elected official was beside the point; the threat was expressive of Tuck's determination not to be outdone by the times, out-of-joint or not. Everybody around him was "dying of the can'ts," he grumbled.

The Governor held it contrary to public interest for public utility workers to strike, and therefore, by invoking the law under which every able-bodied man can be drafted into the militia in an emergency, he arranged to put all the strikers under martial law.

The dispute was settled before the draft into the mythical militia, but a little later, when the General Assembly met in special session to raise teacher salaries, Tuck procured an arsenal of weapons: the Right to Work Act, the Public Utility Labor Relations Act under which the State can take over and operate utilities on the verge of a walkout, and a law to prohibit mass picketing.

One way or another, while America was a Gulliver prone with strikes, Tuck kept buses running, maintained telephone service, and seized a strip mine in Buchanan County to assure a graded supply of fuel for home furnaces during the nation-wide coal strike.

With the other hand he was increasing teacher salaries and upgrading mental hospitals. To support it all, he wangled a sharp general tax increase in 1948, despite the suddenly diminishing fervor of the reformers. "When I got out the collection plate," said Tuck, "they all left me."

The Tuckian approach to a problem was a boisterous summer storm with deafening thunder, blinding lightning and driving rains from which the land emerged rejuvenated, all sweet, green, and smiling, and amazed.

What started out, with Tuck's blessing, as the anti-Truman bill to keep the man from Missouri off the ballot wound up by letting nearly anybody get on it. Not long after the General Assembly's anti-Truman gestures the President and the Governor met to receive honorary degrees at the College of William and Mary.

As the two struggled into their caps and gowns, reporters tried to egg them into a dispute.

"Oh, I don't guess we'll fight, will we Governor?" asked Truman.

"Not," replied Tuck, "in these clothes."

Four minutes at the 1952 Democratic National Convention made Governor Battle nationally famous.

He moved, customarily, at an amble, a slow-moving, amiable elephant, but that night in Chicago he was sitting one moment with the Virginia delegation and the next he was half-way to the rostrum, showing his broad back to former Governor Tuck who also, it is said, had in mind making a speech which would, no doubt, have been another Sumter.

"Where's Jawn going?" asked a startled delegate.

"He's going to make just the best speech you ever heard," said Mrs. John Garland Pollard, the national committeewoman.

His speech — invoking Jefferson in whose seat he sat in the State Senate, whose home he could see when the rising sun struck Monticello— saved Virginia from being expelled from the convention for refusing to sign a loyalty oath. It also heartened Adlai Stevenson whose presidential nomination would have been damaged by a Dixie secession.

The Governor's voice hit a crooning, almost evangelical note that satisfied an awed majority of *his* devotion, anyway, to the party's nominees, and they said so in a long, dramatic roll call of the States.

Seldom does a man enjoy such a moment without the fates demanding a balancing abasement, and in 1956 the Virginia delegation's leaders insisted on nominating Battle for President so they could dodge endorsing

Stevenson, the very man whose hide Battle had helped save in 1952.

To a man of Battle's modesty, the nomination was a torment, a nightmare in the steaming afternoon, and he settled himself grimly by the Virginia standard, as if taking a seat in a bucking roller coaster. But the ride was unexpectedly smooth.

Governor Stanley made the most graceful speech of his four years in placing Battle's name before the Convention. Virginia's delegates, clumped in the center of the slowly filling hall, wondered desperately what they would do when time came to demonstrate through its vast reaches. It was one thing for Governor Battle to be embarrassed. But it was quite another for an ordinary mortal to run around screaming and waving a banner in the broad daylight, all exposed, without the clamoring anonymity of a mob.

But when the moment to demonstrate arrived, the great organ began playing *Carry me back to old Virginny,* and the delegation arose and sang, full-throated, and sat down, and the ordeal was over, and it was all right.

Throughout the rest of the day and that night, delegates from all across the country made their way to the Virginia standard to shake Battle's hand and say, "We wish it was so, Governor." Battle smiled his crooked smile, and his face was tracked, silently, with tears.

All in all, 1956, though less celebrated, was an even better year than 1952.

Governor Stanley holds the record for brevity in campaign promises. At his Inauguration in 1954 he broke a major campaign commitment by asking for a one-cent gas tax increase. It brought howls from the public and press, and was, quite probably, one of his finest hours.

Between his election and the inauguration, Stanley studied highway needs and concluded his anti-tax stand was wrong. Platoons of politicians implored him not to switch. "At least wait until after mid-term," they pleaded. "Let the people forget."

But Stanley persisted, and knowingly invoked a storm on his awkward, honest head. The General Assembly's refusal to raise the tax was the beginning of the end of an effective pay-as-you-go program. The State plunged deeper into the toils of tolls to build tunnels, bridges, and even major highways.

Pay-as-you-go is an austere code requiring Spartan fortitude of politicians. The test came when Governor Stanley stood in the rain and said he had been wrong. Too few could match his humility and statesmanship on that issue.

A trying reassessment also came to J. Lindsay Almond Jr. when, with public schools closed in three Virginia communities, he steered Virginia into a freedom of choice program to comply with court-decreed desegregation. Once he got into the fight he enjoyed it, he said later, and felt he had done the right thing. But it was an emotional wrench, and the roughest was with Senator Byrd Sr. whose impassive resistance delayed Almond's appointment to a Federal court until long after he had left the Mansion.

Few could keep pace for long with the oratorical thunder of Governor Almond, who had been at it ever since he was a boy in Orange County, minding big bronze turkey gobblers in the sun-splashed woods, declaiming to the trees and birds, a rural Demosthenes.

Even as he mounted the steady piston stroke of long sentences and many-syllabled words, his mind was running ahead to search for just the right image or bright hyperbole. He had an almost Dickensian sense of the comic, and, like Dickens when creating, was apt to get caught up in the gusto of what he was doing.

"If Richard Nixon comes in Capitol Square," he once roared, "Thomas Jefferson will turn over in his grave at such a rate that he will hereafter be known as Jumpin' Jeff or Tumblin Tom!" (Among those

Battle

Stanley

Almond

70

who appreciated the Governor's rolling periods was John F. Kennedy who would pause in making notes on the platform and cock his head, smiling, while Almond spoke.) In the midst of the turmoil over school desegregation, Governor Almond managed to put together a most progressive budget for state needs in 1960, predicated forthrightly on a sales tax, which he announced dramatically as "a bare bones budget," almost as if parading Oliver Twist before the populace with sharp ribs and elbows raw and red beneath the rags. As opposition stiffened to his request, he declared he had cut the bare bones budget "to the very marrow," and he heartened his troops with the vow that "we will fight to the last ditch, and dig another ditch."

My last glimpse of Governor Almond in office occured during his ride with Albertis S. Harrison Jr. in the back seat of an open limousine during the inaugural parade for Governor Harrison. You'd have thought their roles were reversed—that Almond, waving to the crowd and laughing, his top hat at a jaunty angle on his white mane, was on his way into office, and Harrison, impassive and meditative, was a lame duck leaving the Mansion with somewhat uncertain prospects.

As I was marveling at the contrast, the parade paused, Governor Almond saw me, and I waved. He waved back, but that did not suffice, because he then clasped his hands above his head and shook them, beaming, and, finally, as the parade began to roll again. he assumed for an instant the pose of a prize fighter, his right fist shoved out, his left tucked under his slightly lowered chin (his top hat tilting forward a bit, too), and that, so far as I was concerned was the way he went out of office, irresistible.

My attention was so gripped by Governor Almond's pantomime that I did not catch Harrison's reaction to this high-spirited wig-wagging between his seat-mate and a reporter, if, indeed, the new Governor saw it at all, because when I became aware of him again, he still seemed wrapped in weighty introspection.

Among seven successive Governors at mid-20th century, a vast, revolving turntable for the Old Dominion, the Southside produced five, and two of them—Governors Harrison and Mills E. Godwin Jr.—teamed for a fiscal revolution.

Virginia politicians had regarded the sales tax as the "tax of last resort," fated to fade unrealized, forever and forever, like the receding horizon. But leaving office in 1966, Governor Harrison recommended a 2 per cent state-wide sales, plus another one per cent to take effect in 1968. Incoming Governor Godwin endorsed the package, so that by the time the localities had tacked on another one per cent, Virginia had a 4 per cent sales tax.

The chief beneficiary of this sudden, if belated, largess was public education. Each Governor had managed to make some contribution to the cause. (Even during World War II, Governor Darden had wrung a million dollars out of the General Assembly in pioneering visual aid, which some legislators endorsed, no doubt, as eyeglasses.) But the great breakthrough had to wait on the sales tax.

Education had become a refrain during the Harrison administration, but there is always the possibility in Virginia that in talking so much about what has to be done, we will fall under the pleasant delusion we have already done it. The Harrison-Godwin tandem operation gave the State, at long last, the money to do it. In October, 1966, Governor Godwin called together a state-wide conference to impart some direction to the spending. It stirred evangelical enthusiasm.

Harrison

Godwin

WATERING THE TREE

Thomas Jefferson remarked that the tree of liberty required an occasional watering by the blood of martyrs. No one could run against Armistead L. Boothe—as did Godwin in 1961 for Lieutenant Governor or Harry F. Byrd Jr. in 1966 for the U. S. Senate—without enlarging his understanding of Virginia.

And for years Delegate Robert Whitehead of Lovingston edified the entire House of Delegates. He was only average in height, even slightly stooped, as he hurried across Capitol Square carrying a bulging brief case, but when he made a point in debate before the podium in the center aisle, he would clinch his fist and swing his right arm up and down as if flaying the backs of the majority. His point finished, he would rear back, his great oven mouth snapped shut and turned down at the corners, a lank white cowlick falling across his forehead, his blue-gray eyes glaring.

When another member dared ask if the Delegate from Lovingston would yield for a question, Whitehead would draw himself up proudly like a duellist and cry, "I yield!"

He yielded to a question as if drawing a sword. And gave, usually, more than he got, a D'Artagnan in debate.

When a defeated bill reappeared in slightly different dress, Whitehead would tag it: "That's just the same old 'coon with another ring around its tail."

In 1950 he demonstrated the State treasury had an extra $2 million that should go to teachers. The House of Delegates agreed, but the State

Senate spread it among other agencies, and when the amended version passed, Whitehead took the center aisle and said, sadly: "I shook the tree, but somebody else picked up the apples."

When most of his colleagues were predicting wondrous results from the Resolution of Interposition, Whitehead said: "The lightning flashed, the thunder crashed—and a chigger died!"

And when a delegate tried to disguise a bad bill under verbiage, Whitehead told him, "You can call it a wampus, but it's still a polecat."

In 1949, campaigning for Francis Pickens Miller for Governor, he collapsed after a broadcast. "It was for the cause, without any compensation," said Miller. "He worked for me harder than he worked for himself. He risked more for me than he would in his own behalf."

(During that 1949 campaign, Miller predicted a huge State budget surplus which, after his defeat, the General Assembly appropriated as school building funds during Governor Battle's administration. The peppery Colonel called them "Battle School Construction Funds for Miller Memorials.")

Lieutenant Governor A. E. S. Stephens waged a rousing, if losing, fight for Governor in 1961, aimed, he said, at restoring the Organization to the era of flexibility when he, Battle, and Darden liked its general philosophy but had their scraps in the legislature without inviting political reprisals.

After the campaign when Stephens was recovering from an illness. I wondered if defeat had slaked his great gusto and dropped him a note. It hadn't. In reply the big, blunt man who had tried to upset the Organization's applecart sent a message in the form of a package from his own yard at Pleasant Point: four tiny, green, sour apples.

Republican Ted Dalton gave the Organization in 1953 "the closest call we ever had," said Senator Byrd. "Until he made that speech he was as good as elected."

Dalton's way was to take an issue, decide where the right lay, and stand there. Two weeks before the close of the 1953 gubernatorial race, he proposed a road bond issue of $100 million, secured by gas tax receipts, but bonds were bonds to Byrd, and he came flying into the campaign, wattles flaming, spurs flashing, and turned it, just barely.

At the opening of the 1954 General Assembly, when the tall, silver-haired State Senator from Radford strode into the chamber, the entire

Whitehead   *Dalton*

Senate, most of them Democrats, stood and applauded as Dalton hurried, red-faced, to his seat.

Byrd said he'd never seen anybody like Dalton. The two of them, chiefs of their respective parties, would hunt together before the 1953 campaign, and Dalton, spying a man working in a field miles across the valley on another mountain-side, would go striding over to talk with him and shake his hand.

In 1958, when Dalton was appearing before the Senate Judiciary Committee for a Federal judgeship, the two met in a corridor and Dalton, in his jovial way, hailed Byrd as the man who had defeated him in 1953.

"Oh, no, Ted," said Byrd, "you beat yourself."

In 1957 Dalton challenged the Organization again in running for Governor against Attorney General Almond. But before the campaign got well underway, the General Assembly members gathered at Jamestown for a swank reception, as they do annually, and Almond and Dalton met, with photographers swarming around for a picture of the two. The Attorney General had just asked for a glass of water, and still held the glass in his hand, a pose that would have outraged the drys in Virginia. But just before the photographers snapped the picture, Dalton held up his hand and called, "Wait, boys!", and turning to the Attorney General, he said, "Lindsay, don't you want to put down that glass?" Almond stuck the glass behind his back, the flash bulbs popped, the two opponents shook hands, and Almond, turning, saw the reporters, and, blurted: "I always said he was one grand-d-d fellow!"

And, though they were not Governors, and losers only once, there

75

must be room for two veterans, one being United States Senator A. Willis Robertson, who flourished oak-like in politics without the semblance of a machine, only a host of friends and admirers. Indeed, when the Organization tried to purge him in 1952, Senator Robertson, riding with a newsman on an evening's journey, was moved to tell him how every time he received a letter or telephone call of support, all of them spontaneous and unsolicited, he took a pin and marked his backer's residence on the wall map in his office.

You'd be surprised, he said, at the pins on that map.

His feel for the past recalled John Smith's saying that "historie is the memory of time." His favorite story concerned the campaign when Col. Robert Toombs of Georgia was running for office after the Civil War.

A constituent interrupted Toombs in mid-flight and said, "Col. Toombs, when you were urging Georgia to secede from the Union, didn't you say we could beat the Yankees with cornstalks."

"Yes, my friend," said the Colonel, "I did make that statement, but the damnyankees wouldn't fight us with cornstalks."

The other veteran told few, or no stories, but Representative Howard W. Smith made history with the bills that died in his Rules Committee, as well as those released to life on the floor. He was tall, thin, and wavering, almost wispy, a gray wraith among the stolid, solid ranks of the House.

He seldom made a speech, and, when he did, he leaned on the podium, his hands clasped along the top edge as if it were a surfboard, and he talked reluctantly, his voice fading at the most dramatic point, as if he shrank from putting the well-known facts of legislative life into words.

Tall, swaying, courtly, his eyes intent, peering from under tangled brows and behind big glasses, he is as distinguished as the praying mantis, that quiet, long-bodied insect that walks on its hind legs with its front claws clasped silently before it, piously, as if in prayer; it moves softly, almost unseen, because it blends into its surroundings, changing from dull green to brown to gray, but when this gentlemanly creature, sometimes called the walking stick, pounces, there is no escaping for its prey. Then praying mantis takes on a new, sinister, preying slant.

At least, that's how he looks to liberals.

The conservatives sometimes called him "Byrd's brains."

In Virginia politics, in the beginning there was Byrd.

And the word was Byrd's.

KING ON THE MOUNTAIN

From childhood Harry F. Byrd was a doer. Of the three Byrd brothers, Winchester townspeople remember Tom's squatting on the sidewalk, looking up dark-eyed to explain, gravely, that he was feeding sugar to the ants; Dick's exploring Valley caves, and Harry's leading the West Enders against the Tater Hill gang and assigning two of his Organization to assist stout Tom in retreat.

But Harry's childhood—and formal education—was short. At 15, bored "by two old women who talked about nothing but the Civil War," he left school to revive the family's newspaper, the *Star*. At 18 he began planting orchards, and soon was managing the local telephone agency, and directing the Valley Turnpike Company. His interest in roads led him to the State Senate at 27 and the Governor's chair at 38.

The former toll road operator managed and helped finance the successful pay-as-you-go campaign for good roads in 1923. The next year Bishop Cannon, drover of the drys, told him he'd have to wait to run for Governor, the first of many dares that fired Byrd to fury, and victory.

Virginia couldn't remember a Governor like him.

He ran the Commonwealth as if it was as much his personal responsibility as the plantation that had been the charge of William Byrd II; and with scant concern for his dress, as he put on whatever came to his hurried hand in the morning and wore it straight through the day, at his desk, in town, or on a mountain.

He had a whole state to set straight. He rushed Virginia, as breathless as a girl going to her first ball, into the 20th century. He gave the Old Dominion a new deal before the New Deal.

He was at his blazing meridian. (About then, Winston Churchill, in political eclipse, visited him, and at the parting of the two cherubic bulldogs, the Briton waved away Byrd's forecast of a great future, and growled: "All that's behind me now.")

Byrd's administration abolished dozens of bureaus and hundreds of superfluous jobs in forming 12 departments, investigated insurance, telephone, and freight rates, reformed the fee system, separated sources of state and local tax revenues, buried sectionalism, raised teacher salaries, installed the short ballot, realized a surplus, modernized the Constitution, and ended lynching with a law that made participation in a mob equivalent to murder.

Virginia, he showed, is not averse to progress.

In his first vote in the United States Senate in 1933 on a bill, prophetically, "To Preserve the Credit of the United States Government," he supported President Roosevelt's request to cut all appropriation 15 per cent, very nearly the last thing on which they agreed.

The President began spending and Byrd, appalled at the rising debt, shifted from offensive to defensive. In a stunning transition, the doer on the Virginia scene became the opposer in the Washington arena, a national symbol of conservatism, an immovable rock in the centralizing whirlpool.

In the 1950's he resisted the Supreme Court's desegregation decrees, and was unshakable in deeming them unconstitutional and unworkable. "I'm either right or I'm wrong," he said, "and I'll be judged by time."

His reforms in Richmond also streamlined officialdom into a more maneuverable campaign vehicle, and that, along with the fact that its strength was as the strength of ten because its heart was pure, made the Organization very nearly invincible. It seldom lost, and never for long.

("Don't ever cross my boy Harry," his father said. "He has the face of an angel and the heart of a tiger!")

The Organization's opponent closed his day with a foreboding that if Byrd slept, he dreamed in terms of wards and precincts. On election day, the Senator called Byrd-men about the State for predictions, trying to pry into the future.

Next day he pored over the returns, district by district, and called around to see how his candidates had fared, an old hen hawk fussing over her rapacious brood.

For weeks he played over the campaign's moves, exploring every road untaken in the yellow wood.

Even climbing mountains he picked his way in his mind through political problems, or talked to a parade of politicians, strung out panting behind him, the mountainside tilted before them like an opened book, which Byrd read while they sweated.

His landslide of recollections of bouts with Presidents ("Something about the job makes a man resent disagreement," said Byrd) was mixed in his hearers' memories with the tracery of twigs and leaves and jumbled boulders from which they dared not lift their eyes; or, if they did, once or twice, it was only to glimpse the bobbing back of Byrd's head and the small bald spot, ember-red, amid the frosty fringe of hair. At the top, they flopped, dazed, benumbed by the mountain and the man.

A scoutmaster, leading his patrol down the steep side of Hawksbill, came upon the senator toiling up alone, and stored the glimpse of old Byrd in his natural habitat, cane in hand, blue shirt plastered wet to his chest, face fiery, blue eyes beaming on the clustering boys.

Once, hiking with my boys, he fascinated them with lore on bears,

—Photograph by James Netherwood

such as the fact that the black bear can climb a tree and the grizzly can't, and as he talked, we came to a spreading patch of blueberries, and now and then Byrd would reach down and grab a berry, and, gradually, he slowed his walk and his talk, and strayed off the trail, as did the rest of us, until finally, when I looked up, we were scattered around like bears eating berries, silently, voraciously, in the sun on top of Old Rag.

When he chose not to talk, no one could draw him out. One day, in 1960, Lyndon Johnson, John F. Kennedy and George Smathers trooped to his Senate office to beard the limping old bear in his den and win his endorsement.

As Johnson talked, Byrd grew more remote, drawing into himself, slipping further and further away, his eyes increasingly abstract, his voice dropping off, finally so faint and tiny that the three had to bend to catch it, just as on a summer's day, the Blue Ridge mountains have a trick of fading into nothingness, as if you could walk right through the wavery, misty wall of them, until, at last, it was almost as if Byrd wasn't there, and even Lyndon Johnson found he was talking into thin air and gave up. Throughout, Smathers sat silent, amazed, and Kennedy, amused.

That summer at his annual orchard picnic, Byrd, clad in white, climbed onto an orange, flat-bed truck. From behind green, stacked cans of applesauce, he spoke to applegrowers, politicians, and neighbors seated on clean, white crates scattered through the sloping grove of towering hardwoods.

"When I want to speak out, I do, and when I don't, I DON'T," he shouted in his strident, hawk's scream. "I have found that sometimes silence is golden."

He read his oath to support and defend the Constitution. "That's my platform. That's what I try to do," he said. "These parties come and go. Some are conservative, some are radical, but the Constitution remains, and the oath that I have taken is my platform."

Easy generosity marked his personal relations. He declined government subsidies on his orchards and insisted on a change in the Kennedy tax bill that cost him a windfall. At the winding entrance to Rosemont is a sign: *Visitors Welcome.* Tourists picnic casually amid the pink and white dogwood. Another sign, *Watch Out for The Dog,* did not mean beware but take care and don't run over the black cocker spaniel—a needless sign, really, because Candy stuck like a small shadow at his master's heels, trailing him once, even, onto the floor of the Senate. ("We like you *and* your dog, Harry," said Vice-President Nixon, "but he really oughtn't to come onto the floor.")

He dotted the ridges around Skyland with stone shelters for climbers caught in the rain as he had been, now and then, going back to when he was 15, and his father had introduced him to the mountains as great restorers. He retreated to them every week-end, and the first thing he did, like an old bear coming home, was to check around the public camping grounds at Big Meadows, a wavy pasture in the sky, his satisfaction mounting as he viewed the campers in the cabins, then those in tents near conveniences, and, finally, the ones way back off the trail, on their own. By that time, he was beaming.

In the spring Byrd had a series of luncheons for fellow senators, Berryville neighbors, and friends from around Virginia. On the broad, pillared porch overlooking the orchards, a hundred or so gathered at the final party, liberal Northeastern senators chatting with Deep South conservatives, Midwest Republicans talking with West Coast Democrats.

Midway, Byrd left the porch and came out, unseen, onto a small second-story balcony and looked down at the throng. Gradually, the guests became aware of his watching them. The talk stilled, some men raised their glasses to him, the women clapped, a rippling of applause, and then, in the intense silence, before he turned and clumped off the balcony, Byrd said, softly, "Finest people I ever saw."

Shortly after, he began to fade. Few knew the will he had to exert to preside over his committee. At last, on Nov. 11, 1965, he resigned I called him from home three evenings later to wish him well. He talked with us and said we would all climb a mountain in the spring. But he still was worrying about giving up.

Over and over, amid mutual assurances that surely we would climb another mountain, he kept asking, almost in stammering eagerness: "Do you think I did the right thing. Did I do right?"

THE TIDES AND THE COAST

The most thorough recent investigation of Virginia was by Dr. Gott-mann, a French economic geographer commissioned by philanthropist Paul Mellon to diagnose the Old Dominion. The doctor took stock of us for 18 months, visiting every county and city, a latter-day Tocqueville, perceptive and balanced in his judgments.

At the conclusion of his research, state officials honored him at lunch-eon in the Hotel Richmond. The geographer had an interesting face, the listening sort, with merry quickness in his features that promised a deft riposte when he chose, a fencer's face.

The meal droned along, the conversation about as distinctive as the mashed potatoes, and, in a lull, I leaned forward and called down the table to ask Dr. Gottmann what impressed him most about America.

"The waste!" he called back.

"I mean," he added, "the creative waste."

Europe, his thesis went, tends to revere things as they are simply be-cause they have always been there. At every turn, a thousand-year-old building bars the way. But Americans, with eyes on the future, do not hesitate to turn a river, level a mountain, fill a canyon, and pull down a skyscraper only recently built to build a bigger one.

"Willingness to change is the outstanding characteristic of America," he said.

As the company was digesting this, I asked what he found to be the outstanding characteristic of Virginia.

82

"Resistance to change," said the little Frenchman, smiling.

He viewed Virginia as an oasis of calm. Perhaps its leisurely way of life had a mission in the mellowing of America, but, fortunately for the Western World, America's Promethean tradition had prevailed.

Now this vignette — a many-layered revelation — was not finished. When Dr. Gottmann concluded his comparison of America and Virginia, our host, a dear person and a department commissioner, nodded his head in sober agreement with Dr. Gottmann, and said quietly, "Yes, in Virginia we like to wait to do a thing until after someone else has tried it first."

The stark remarks at lunch should not be taken as epitomizing the book. Dr. Gottmann found that from a rural state "with a few middle-sized urban nuclei and an altogether modest rank among the states, with the sole exception of historical seniority, Virginia had become in the 1950's one of the most rapidly developing states in the Union, attracting in-migration, highly urbanized, and powerfully industrialized."

This is the eternal pattern, the tides of change beating against the coast of resistance.

What fascinated him was Virginia's determination to go about shaping the changes to her own ways. Industrializing, modern Virginians scattered factories widely to avoid mill towns (repeating the instinct of colonial settlers who declined to cluster in towns but separated among distant plantations, a practice encouraging independence.)

Virginia farmers held onto their acreage and commuted daily to the factory. (Dan River Mills regularly granted two days off during the hog-killing season.)

My question to Dr. Gottmann was an echo of the same inquiry that was put for decades to University of Richmond students by a fiery old history professor, an acute critic of the Virginia scene.

"What is the outstanding characteristic of Virginians?" Dr. Samuel Chiles Mitchell asked each freshman class.

The students, their hands leaping trout-like, suggested this and that, until finally the old teacher wrote in giant letters across one whole panel of the blackboard the word: "REASONABLENESS."

The trait was a hand-me-down from the English. Virginians knocked the "r" off revolution to turn it into evolution.

Whatever you call it—Faulkner's decency, Dr. Gottmann's calm, Dr.

Mitchell's reasonableness—the quality runs through the Virginia character like a great bedrock. And it sustained the state during the school desegregation crisis, much as 100 years earlier it had enabled Virginia, a buffer state between the North and South, to bear most of the fury of the Civil War.

At the height, or the depths, of the troubles—when the school-closing laws shut down public education in Norfolk for a semester — reporters who had surveyed the South predicted that a sense of integrity would help Virginia adjust in relatively good temper to changes that would stir elements elsewhere to violence.

Amid the pulling to and fro of politicians, the people remained calm, a vast, still deep beneath the vexed surface. And when historians take stock of Virginia from the vantage of the year 2000, they likely will discover that as the first half of the 20th Century was closing, the outstanding man in Virginia was the common man. In keeping his head, he set something of an example for the rest of the South, no small service for an oasis.

In his *A Study of History,* Arnold J. Toynbee used Virginia and South Carolina to illustrate his theory of the nemesis of creativity among civilizations: the idea that the leadership that distinguishes itself in dealing with one challenge is apt to fail conspicuously in attempting to deal with the next.

A foreign visitor to the Old South "in the fifth decade of the 20th Century would assuredly pick out Virginia and South Carolina as the two states in which there was least sign of promise of recovery" from the Civil War, he wrote. By contrast, North Carolina had less far to fall, and, unencumbered by a load of laurels, much less difficulty recovering from the shock and picking herself up.

(All this theory is reflected in popular sayings. There's the observation that North Carolina is "the valley of humility between two mountains of conceit." And another that "all a North Carolinian knows is the three r's: "reading, 'riting, and the road to Richmond." Which the North Carolinians reversed by saying that all Virginians know is "the road to Raleigh.")

Dr. Toynbee came to Williamsburg in June, 1961, to speak at the Prelude to Independence ceremonies, and I showed up at his door with his baggage, just after his arrival from the airport. It was late, he was hungry—tea was on the way, it turned out—but he sat down to talk, one of the most forbearing persons I ever met, his large, benign head thrust forward on the frail, stooped scholar's body, almost like a pale, oracular mummer's mask held by a small boy.

His voice had a breathless quality, a hesitancy in speech, as if he were vastly excited over what he was viewing. He had a habit of pausing to check on his companion's reaction—"Don't you think so?"—as if all of us are spectators alike at the grand panorama, on the same footing before its majesty, in a position to teach each other. The pause was something more than a courtesy. He *listened* intently, thirstily, as a child, or Aristotle. How Jefferson would have enjoyed him!

My question was why today's legislatures did not present the dazzling array of genius of the Colonial era, great exploding novae of talent, politics raised to the rank of statecraft.

The amount of genius didn't vary, said Toynbee. In the founding of this nation, politics was the main outlet for talent that is spread today through other attractive and exciting fields. Many business executives are the kind of persons who, 200 years ago, would have made their marks in politics.

"This is serious," he said. "We can't go on making democracy work if to be in politics is considered a kind of third or fourth choice."

Never, he said, has there been such a crop of political genius as this country produced in the Colonial era. Later, it had terrific giants, such as Lincoln, but not the profusion of the founders.

"Your energies become absorbed in economy," he said, in opening the West, building the continent, and developing technology.

The shortage was felt world-wide, said Toynbee, with the possible exceptions of India and the emerging nations of Africa.

His sweeping judgments were exhilarating, but I had a major reservation. Few of the emerging nations present the prospect of much more than chaos. Leadership will continue to come from America, the young, fresh flower of the West, and Virginia will play an ever-enlarging role in national life, something of a resumption of old Colonial glory.

The pace in the Old Dominion has been quickening much faster than Toynbee, or most Virginians, realized. The sudden surge of the 1966 Virginia General Assembly, with break-throughs on several fronts, testifies to it.

But the change has been there all along, if at times subterranean. Is it surprising that the most fought-over state in the Union (one town, Winchester, changed hands 70 times) took a diminished role on the national scene while recovering?

Dr. Gottmann placed the end of reconstruction at about 1915 and lay heavy emphasis on the network of roads which Virginia built in the late 20's and 30's as the avenues of progress. Desegregation consumed our energies for a decade, but, that resolved, we are emerging, stronger than ever, into the sunlight.

The most eloquent testimony to Virginia's future lay all about us, as Dr. Toynbee and I talked, in the golden triangle of history formed by Jamestown, Yorktown, and Williamsburg.

'I WOULD YET BEGIN AGAIN...'

The image of the Cavalier emigre from the scattered court of Charles I pleases many Virginians, but an even earlier, nobler exemplar, one of the mighty, mythic figures of the Western World, is stocky Captain John Smith.

Not only a soldier, he was a creator, first of the line of practical visionaries who strove, and strive, to create a better world of even this brave new world. John Smith, a Prospero between his kind and the red Caliban, wished to keep the two camps in working harmony. He wanted no war there on the thin scythe of civilization facing a wilderness continent.

Old Powhatan, despot of two dozen tribes, sensed that the little soldier was the life force of the colony, and sought, now and then, to test him. John Smith parried and returned the thrusts in measured retaliation. They waged, as Philip L. Barbour describes in *The Three World of Captain John Smith,* a careful cold war.

Time and again, Smith saved the colonists from starvation, from Indians, and from themselves. In the end, a cabal of colonists, not Powhatan, did him in, forcing his return to England. With no Smith to goad them and trade with the Indians, the Starving Time came upon the colonists and cut the population from 500 to 95.

When Smith put down his sword, he picked up his pen in England as a publicist for Virginia and New England. He offered to guide the Pilgrims to the coast he had explored and named. They bought his books and maps but chose another soldier, Miles Standish.

(That must have disappointed John Smith but then how wretched would have been his fate to escape the axe of Powhatan, thanks to Pocahontas, only to fall into the domestic clutches of Priscilla and wind up embalmed in the honeyed iambics of Henry Wadsworth Longfellow.)

Not even Pocahontas could woo him from his purpose. In the pursuit of a greater romance, a grander passion—colonization—there was no room for domesticity, no time for apron strings in a jostling career of exploring, map-making, trading, and fighting, and, in the end, writing.

He put it best, late in his life's twelfth hour, when trying to arouse others to the attractions of Virginia and New England, he wrote:

"By that acquaintance I have with them, I may call them my children; for they have been my wife, my hawks, my hounds, my cards, my dice, and in total my best content, as indifferent to my heart as my left hand to my right: and notwithstanding all those miracles of disaster [which] have crossed both them and me, yet were there not one Englishman remaining (as God be thanked there is some thousands) I would yet begin again with as small means as I did at first."

Catch, will you, the gusto of the man in speaking of his *"miracles* of disaster,"

Ready to begin again. . .

He was the first Virginian, the first American. . .

John Smith.

(And what an American name, a miracle of plainness, for the first American!)

And here at Jamestown was where it all began.

The Stockade is an especial delight to children, but even better is the simple, wonderful sight of the coast, low and gray across the water, just as John Smith saw it when he lifted his eyes from the problem at hand. At the glimpse of that line of shore, unchanged, you feel a thrill of recognition at what the settlers felt in the raw, cold winter and hot, festering summer. The other moving wonder is the ruined tower of the old church, a shard, but still cupping in its thick, broken walls a stillness of the time that was.

Yorktown—where Cornwallis, the most gallant of foes, surrendered —and Jamestown and Williamsburg form the cradle of the nation. ("Go down there and put your hand on it!" my teacher thundered. "You can rock it.")

And it is, indeed, still rocking, still producing ideas, aspirations, and courses of action.

Every American, and foreign visitor, should walk the mile down the Duke of Gloucester Street between the College of William and Mary and the Capitol.

It is the main street, the mainstream, of American history.

Among those who took the walk was John D. Rockefeller Jr. in the company of the Rev. W. A. R. Goodwin of Bruton Parish Church.

And as they walked down the still, moonlit street, the minister unfolded to the philanthropist his dream of restoring Williamsburg to all her old, fresh glory.

"It was," said Mr. Rockefeller, "the most expensive walk in history."

Often, the financier returned to take the walk alone when the only sound was the scrape of a leaf across a moon-softened stone step or the creaking of the signboard on the Raleigh Tavern, from which might burst at any moment, arm in arm, Washington, Wythe, and Jefferson, intoxicated with ideas.

And if the insatiably curious Jefferson returned, he would be fascinated with Williamsburg, and not only because of the recapitulation of the physical past.

The unexpected quality lies not in the restored buildings to captivate the eye, but in the revival of the Revolutionary spirit to stimulate the mind.

It is a stirring, hopeful irony that sweet Virginia, brooding amid the wreaths of her past, should find arising in the Old Capital the eagerness to greet the future that characterized the Founding Fathers.

Jefferson might be startled momentarily at confronting a tourist in an orange, blue-flowered sports shirt, bedecked, argus-eyed, with cameras, but, wandering into the House of Burgesses, (where as a William and Mary student he listened, and marveled at Patrick Henry crying Freedom!), he would again be stirred to hear foreign students from all over the world debate the day's issues at the annual Williamsburg International Assembly.

Then, indeed, he would know that he was home, and the Revolution he had sired was still going on.

The International Assembly—a last chance to bring together foreign graduate students to swap impressions of America, the only debriefing that most of them get—is one of dozens of intellectual contests (symposiums, seminars, and assemblies) which animate and add a new dimension to the buildings: *meaning*. Thus is the Revolution restored to the fullest, the architecture of the mind as well as mansions.

Or consider the excitement of Patrick Henry if he could have watched the gathering of high school student leaders from the 50 states along with foreign exchange students, in the spring of 1966 to discuss: "Protest—a right and a responsibility."

How the blue-eyed wordsmith who forged the war cries of the Revolution would have loved to appear on the panel as an expert on protests before the annual Student House of Burgesses!

So rich a role does Williamsburg play in the nation's life that the State Department arranges for foreign rulers to get their first vital impression of the United States by spending the night of their arrival at the Colonial Capital.

The experiment that started with John Smith and flowered with Thomas Jefferson surpassed any creative endeavor the world has known, greater than Greece because it practiced what Greece only theorized, grander than Rome because its ideals shone, instead of dimming, in use.

The Founding Fathers had a buoyant faith in themselves, their God, and their country's destiny. They did not fear change. They embraced it as a friend and shaped it to their ends. They knew that change is the great constant. Change is growth, change is life, and, guided creatively, change is within the purpose of God. It is with us, sweeping toward us like a wave, whether or not we like. We had best, as they did, meet change joyfully, zestfully, masterfully.

That is the lesson of Williamsburg yesterday and today. It is, more than her kindest critics sense, the story of Virginia tomorrow. She is responding, swifter than they realize, to the tempo of the challenge of the times, ready to take her rightful place in the family of states, the wise mother, the creative mother, the producer of ingenious offspring, breeder of ideas, guide to a nation.

That's what it is about Virginia.

*   *   *   *

'IT IS NOT ENOUGH TO SURVIVE'

As I began revising this second edition of "What Is It About Virginia?", my mind turned in 1974 to Dr. Jean Gottmann, the French geographer, whom I interviewed in 1955 after he finished analyzing Virginia. He viewed the State as an oasis of calm that might offer the nation a lesson in leisurely living; but fortunately for the Western World, he said, America's promethean dedication to progress had prevailed.

Still, in his book "Virginia at Mid-Century" he noted that the "old partitions show more and more cracks" in Virginia under the impact of industrialization and urbanization. "This trend," he wrote, "makes for change although it cannot prevent new sets of partitions from arising."

In 1969 after three field trips to Virginia, Dr. Gottmann revised his book under a new title "Virginia in Our Century." His second look was as perceptive as the first. Changes had proceeded faster and gone deeper than he had anticipated. At times, he wrote, "the will to change seems so striking as to make an observer wonder whether the whole tradition and way of life of Virginia will be at stake in the next few years."

Virginia's economy had expanded spectacularly. But Dr. Gottmann found even more dramatic changes in attitudes, especially in Virginians' desire to improve education "at all levels for all their people."

If the changes are many, "the preservation of past tradition and landscape is even more important. But the visitor feels more fluidity and soul-searching than he used to perceive."

In the continuing struggle beteen old ideals and new ideas, he wrote, the Virginians' sense of tradition gives them an "appreciation of the quality of their way of life. As they keep endeavoring to catch up with the more advanced sections of the country, they remain more conscious than most Americans are of the qualitative side of things. They want to equal the quantitative achievements of others but hesitate to do so at the cost of the qualitative aspects of their physical and social environment."

Trying to catch up with the present and keep hold of the best of the past, "Virginia may bring to America one more great contribution if she succeeds in striking a happy balance between security and opportunity, between quantity and quality. In recent years Virginians have made a good start on this path," he concluded.

In March 1971, Dr. Gottmann, now head of Oxford University's department of geography, visited Virginia again, this time purely for pleasure. At a table by a sunny window in the Williamsburg Inn, we discussed changing Virginia.

The first geographer to define Megalopolis, America's "main street" from Boston to Washington, D.C., Dr. Gottmann said his impression was that the urban march had reached Fredericksburg and one day might encompass Richmond and take in Hampton Roads. Another offshoot was pushing out of the Northern Virginia suburbs toward the Blue Ridge and Charlottesville.

In the 1969 edition of his book, I noted, his view on Virginia's leisurely style seemed to have shifted to one of approval. Did he now feel it fortunate that Virginia had not moved at the Nation's rapid cadence?

"You are quite right! You are quite right! In a way, if I may say so, on two short visits to Virginia since I revised the book, I also felt that a great deal of Virginia — not the heart but many parts of it — had become less Virginian. Partly this was because of in-migration of people from the outside — some of them coming precisely to take advantage of opportunity that had not been fully exploited by the local people and others because it was a nice country in which to live. But today, at least in Northern Virginia, one hears much less the Virginia accent."

Did he feel a sense of regret at Virginia's quickening development?

There was a long pause and then he said, "Well, I suppose I'm probably getting a little old myself, looking back to younger and older times. But on the other hand the Virginia people are probably better off now. That's what counts for them."

But even as they are becoming better off, I said, Virginia is stepping up development when the rest of the country is talking about slowing down and people are questioning the virtues of unbridled industrialization.

"And, of course," said Dr. Gottmann, "people of good sense are beginning to ask questions all over our Western World. And it is necessary that we do not let the machine and other technological innovations dominate our lives too much.

"It's not necessarily a question of survival," he said. "I'm one of those who feels that when it comes to survival, men will do whatever is necessary to survive. But it's not enough to survive. We still want the good life, and for that we do not always act as we should; and part of it is a matter of too much ambition and drive to go too fast for the opportunity that improved technology provides."

What did he regard as the good life?

"I don't mean only the better condition of the environment. I mean also a more relaxed life of the individual. I mean also more brotherhood, more interest in human relations, not simply to avert criminality but to actually enjoy the smile of the chap you meet."

What area of Virginia did he most enjoy?

"I like very much the mountains, and not only the landscape but I was attracted — perhaps only because I was a visitor for a brief period — by some of the virtues of the less promethean parts.

"Then I like this area, the historic Peninsula. I must say that now that Williamsburg has grown so large, it's more difficult to feel that you are not in a crowd. But, of course, others have the right to enjoy Williamsburg, too. I have enjoyed it for many years in the past. What am I still doing here?"

Colonial Williamsburg's staff, trying to ease the crowding, is constantly unearthing new attractions, I noted, but to keep the charm and yet accommodate the increasing numbers the charm draws is a problem.

What, I asked, had prompted philanthropist Paul Mellon to commission Dr. Gottmann to diagnose Virginia?

"A sense of duty, I think, and also a very warm affection for the state. Only after a year or two of work in Virginia did I begin to understand that feeling."

What is it about Virginia that inspires such feeling? I asked.

After another long pause, he replied: "It is very difficult to say, you know, because one is analyzing oneself. Partly of course, it's that the state is so beautiful. Partly it is a very warm and kind population you have had here. And it's also probably a feeling that in a way Virginians are a people who have been trying to do certain things that they feel they haven't quite been able to do. There is a certain humility about Virginians which is attractive."

That was the first time anybody ever described Virginians as being humble, I observed.

"I know, I know, I know! But my impression is that although they are proud of the beauty of the countryside and of the Presidents and other great men they have produced, there's a certain deep-seated and rather often expressed attitude of not having succeeded in what they wished to do. Whether this was a sort of hangover from the defeat of the Civil War or whether it was something more deep-seated, I don't know.

"There is a deep element of idealism in the Virginians. It may not be that of every person, but there is no country, no people that is idealistic from top to bottom. It is a matter of whether there is a certain leadership and a certain number of people that have it."

I suggested that the Revolutionary period, not the Civil War, enthralls many Virginians. They look to the Founding Fathers and to Williamsburg.

"Here is the Revolution to them," I said. "This is the intellectual—"

"The debating ground for a great deal of the philosophy of the 18th century," he broke in.

"Yes sir," I said, "I think they sometimes look to Williamsburg—"

"—which is taking some of the very best ideas that came out of 18th century liberal England," Dr. Gottmann finished.

It seemed to me that after the Civil War, we lost the way, I said.

"Well, you had greatly suffered during the war and it takes quite some time to recover," he said.

"But the Civil War and the Reconstruction isn't as troubling as what we failed to do in our own time — from the 1930s up to the early 1960s. It's only lately we've got back on the track," I said. "There hadn't been the vision that prevailed prior to the Civil War. Or maybe the light went out along with the founding fathers."

That's how the conversation went in 1971.

Holton   *Howell*

And now, at this writing in 1974, the Nation's promethean thrust has helped produce an energy crisis. Will Virginia's leadership recoil from that challenge and pull back in a shell? Or will it continue to push the search for the good life that an aroused General Assembly began in 1966?

Not even the election in 1969 of the first Republican Governor in a hundred years, Linwood Holton, distracted the heavily Democratic General Assembly. The newness of the experience for the Republicans as well as Virginia was demonstrated two days after the election when Holton walked into the Capitol Building on his way to the Governor's Office on the third floor. Just inside the building, the sandy-haired Holton turned and inquired, "How do you get there?"

Once there, nobody enjoyed being Governor as much as he did. Each morning he awakened his two sons in the Mansion by shouting as he burst into their room, "Opportunity time! Opportunity time!" Whatever his sons may have thought of that clarion cry, it was how the first Republican Governor greeted the day — and problems.

He pledged to help make Virginia a model of race relations, and he and Mrs. Holton contributed personally to that goal by enrolling their children in integrated public schools. The image of his administration that will prove the most lasting was the photograph of the Governor of Virginia accompanying his daughter to her new school. The projects begun in

96

the Godwin Administration continued, as in 1970 Virginians approved by 2 to 1 a newly revised, progressive Constitution.

The Democrats' bright hope was Lieutenant Governor J. Sargeant Reynolds, who had been elected in 1969. But in August 1970 he was stricken with a brain tumor. He worked heroicly as if his brilliant future were unclouded, but died, only 34 years of age, in June 1971.

The three-way race to replace Reynolds was won by a Democrat running as an independent, Norfolk Senator Henry Howell. An irrepressible populist, Howell cried, "It's easy to make history in Virginia!" Too much legislation favored corporate interests, he insisted, and he meant to right the balance.

In running as an independent, Howell followed the example, if not the philosophy, of conservative U. S. Senator Harry F. Byrd Jr., who left the House of His Fathers to win re-election in 1970. In 1972 the Democrats suffered a heavy loss in the defeat of moderate Senator William B. Spong Jr. by ultraconservative Republican William Scott.

Then in 1973 Mills Godwin, who had presided as a Democratic Governor over four years of creative change from 1966 to 1970, switched to the Republican Party and narrowly defeated Henry Howell for Governor. While Virginians were returning the former Byrd lieutenant to the Governor's chair they also elected the sons of the Byrd Organization's chief

Dalton

Reynolds

Miller

challengers of the 1950s. Democrat Andrew Miller, son of Francis Pickens Miller, won another term as Attorney General, and John Dalton, son of Ted Dalton who had built the modern, moderate Republican Party, won a three-way race for Lieutenant Governor. Waiting to take the oath of office, young John Dalton looked across the Inaugural stands at his father. "Ted should have been doing this 20 years ago," remarked the son. "But what he did then made it a lot easier for me."

Confronted by the energy crisis, the 1974 General Assembly sputtered and stalled. It did provide funds to reform Virginia's barbaric prisons. But it postponed more than 200 pieces of legislation and killed a dozen worthy measures, including a land-use bill aimed at saving vestiges of the countryside in which Virginians take pride. A bill for a proposed bond issue for state parks was not even introduced.

Could the General Assembly regain its progressive stride? And, in trying to cope with increasing population and rising costs, could local and state governments continue to function efficiently and honestly? Could Virginia's integrity survive modern day wheeling and dealing?

These were questions uppermost as Virginia prepared to observe the 200th birthday of the Nation her sons had founded.

PEANUTS AND PAST RECOLLECTIONS
(Update: Spring, 1983)

Virginians are not above recognizing their frailties. Witness a question that surfaced in the 1980s: "How many Virginians does it take to change a light bulb?"

"Three," was the reply. "One to put in the new bulb and two to tell how good the old one was."

The lure of the past is powerful. There's so much to look back to. First, the creative American Revolution that gave a nation the words to live by. No other era has known so many individuals of genius and vision. Then the Civil War, with plumes and swords and unbelievable casualties as wonderfully brave and woefully misled youths rushed massed artillery. In a single engagement west of Petersburg, too obscure to bear a name other than "the fighting along White Oak Road," 10,000 fell.

Then came the grim Reconstruction, followed by recurring hard times culminating in the Great Depression. In those dreary days, the impulse was to glory in the great Revolutionary figures and romanticize the terrible Civil War. "We lived on peanuts and past recollections," a Southampton County farmer told me.

Enamored though many Virginians may seem with the past, their government sometimes does little to preserve the best of it. Many lovely old houses have gone under the bulldozer's tread. Similarly, although Virginians have an almost mystical attachment to the land, the General Assembly hasn't appropriated a cent to buy state parks since 1968. Fortunately, the land has fared far better with the private donors.

In 1965 the Virginia Outdoors Recreation Commission, led by former State Senator FitzGerald Bemiss, proposed adding 36 parks to the nine established with federal funds in the 1930s. Governor Holton endorsed plans for a bond issue of $87 million. With the onset of the Recession in 1973 Governor Godwin began to retrench, and the Commission reduced the proposed bond issue to $18 million. Then the General Assembly cut it to $5 million and removed the most vital provision: funds to buy sites for parks. Well into the 1980s the state had acquired only a dozen additional parks. Four of those were private donations, inspired in part by the Commission's master plan.

In a small beginning with great consequences, 65,000 Virginians checked off on their 1981 state income tax forms the withholding of modest amounts from their refunds to be used for nongame wildlife. Their donations, averaging $6, brought $370,000, which, matched for federal grants, swelled to $602,000. The funds support such causes as propagation of endangered species—eagles, ospreys, peregrine falcons—under the dirction of Mitchell Byrd of William and Mary College.

State Senator William F. Parkerson Jr., who introduced the check-off bill with Delegate Wayne O'Bryan as its House sponsor, said it was vital that some funds be set aside for saving critical habitats as well as endangered species. Dr. Byrd's work demonstrates the great deal one person can do in saving wildlife from extinction, Parkerson observed. Still, it makes little sense to bring back eagles if they can find no place to nest on Virginia's rapidly shrinking shore.

Private donors also led in preserving the Dismal Swamp. Union Camp Corporation gave 49,000 acres in 1973. Gifts from Weyerhaeuser raised the total to 57,565 acres. North Carolina set aside 14,300 acres, and the U.S. Department of the Interior aims to raise the total to 109,000 for a national wildlife refuge. One can still see butterflies in Old Dismal.

The Nature Conservancy foundation rescued another fragile legacy by buying 13 barrier islands off Virginia's coast for migrating waterfowl. Even as the Swamp and coastal islands were being saved, an environmental nightmare unfolded in July 1975. State investigators discovered that Kepone had drained into the James River at Hopewell from Life Science Products Co., which manufactured the highly toxic pesticide for Allied Chemical Corporation. The corporation paid a heavy fine and made a large gift for the environment. No one could foresee when the James, which winds through so much of Virginia and its history, would again run clean. With human life and wildlife imperiled, the need for anti-pollution controls for Virginia's environment would seem beyond question.

Signals at the close of the 1970s suggested that Virginia's very integrity, its most prized possession, might not be invulnerable and had best not be taken for granted. Although, under Harry Byrd's Organization, Virginians might economize on every other aspect of government, they brooked no compromises or short cuts in its honesty. But Virginians, it developed in the 1970s, were among highway contractors convicted of bid-rigging in a 16-state region. And a probe of the State's division of purchases and supply resulted in the conviction of one division official for accepting bribes. Even Virginia's General Assembly, regarded as one of the cleanest state legislatures, pondered questions of conflict of interest.

"Maybe Virginia is not as different as we thought it was," commented former U.S. Senator William B. Spong Jr., now dean of the Marshall-Wythe Law School at William and Mary College. Dean Spong's dry remark brought to mind John Adams' reply when he was asked how Virginians differed from residents of other states. "In Virginia," Adams said, "all the geese think they are swans."

*   *   *   *

Virginians could draw hope from some developments as they entered the 1980s. They approved in 1970 a mildly progressive revision of their State Constitution. It eased pay-as-you-go requirements slightly, but it applied safeguards to even so sensible a reform as having the State back revenue bonds for construction of self-financing projects such as college dormitories and dining halls. The Constitution continued to protect the State's fiscal solvency as fiercely as a duenna chaperoning schoolgirls. And that attitude accounted in part for Virginia being among the states best equipped to weather the deepening recession in 1983.

Often the revisions recognized what already had taken place. Still, playing safe by working well within the realm of the possible and then campaigning vigorously for ratification, Virginia leaders won the voters' approval. In contrast charter changes had failed to carry in seven other states since 1967. Had Virginia's revision occured a year or two later during a slipping economy, it might not have carried by a 3 to 1 ratio or at all. It caught the tide.

The pride of the new Constitution was its concern for public education. It requires that the General Assembly "seek to ensure" a program of high quality. But that word "seek" is a weak one, substituted by the General

Assembly for the Constitutional Commission's forthright "shall." Still a mandate that localities support public schools was a striking advance in Virginia where some schools had been closed during the Depression of the 1930s and resistance to integration in the 1950s.

Along with a new Constitution, Virginians reshaped the state's political structure. For three decades political analysts had talked of Virginia's "emerging two-party system." It seemed to be emerging perpetually as the underdog Republican Party struggled against a powerful Democratic Party dominated by the Byrd Organization. Then between 1970 and 1980 Virginia Republicans elected three successive Governors and two U.S. Senators. They also elected all but one of the state's delegation to the House of Representatives. Though the Democrats still held an overwhelming majority in the General Assembly, Republicans by 1982 had increased their holdings to a third of the membership of the House of Delegates. The competitive two-party system was no longer merely emerging; it had arrived. The public stood to gain from the sharp eye that each party would keep on the other.

Republicans benefited from a decade of suicidal strife between liberals and moderate-conservatives among the Democrats. In 1977 Democrat Henry E. Howell, having defeated Andrew P. Miller in a hard-fought primary, faced Republican John N. Dalton in the November election. The thorough Dalton had put together a strong campaign and, aided by a coalition with former conservative Democrats, he amassed nearly 60 per cent of the vote. When Dalton concluded his oath at the swearing-in at the Capitol's South Portico, he embraced his father, retired U.S. District Judge Ted Dalton. "God bless you," whispered Ted Dalton to the newly inaugurated Governor of Virginia in his arms.

Various Governors have called State government the Commonwealth's biggest business. John Dalton treated it as one. He installed tight budget controls and drafted economies that helped produce a surplus of $150 million in 1980. An air of decisiveness pervaded his administration.

A 10-year dispute between federal and state officials over desegregation of public colleges came to a head early in his term. HEW, prodded by a federal judge, ordered Virginia and other Southern states to step up the pace of desegregation. Dalton came under heavy pressure to confront HEW in court. It posed an interesting test for the young Governor. His father, Ted Dalton, running for Governor in 1957, had challenged the Byrd Organization's Massive Resistance policy of having

Warner and Taylor   *Obenshain*

the State withhold school aid from a locality that permitted integration
in public schools. Among those urging John Dalton to oppose HEW
were former Massive Resisters.

After 10 months of negotiations, Dalton offered in 1979 proposals
to attract more members of each race to the other's colleges and to raise
to a level with those of white colleges the offerings at predominantly black
Virginia State University in Petersburg and Norfolk State University.
The Governor also agreed to reduce programs that were duplicated among
black and white colleges, particularly between Norfolk State and Old
Dominion University. Dalton, an aide said, realized that to attend to other
pressing issues he had to resolve the time-consuming squabble with HEW.
As the state tries to correct inequities deep-rooted through three centuries,
periodic negotiations seem inevitable, especially since many blacks feel
strong bonds with colleges that historically have educated their race.

*   *   *   *

During the Virginia Republican Party's lean years, Democrats used
to jeer that the GOP chose candidates in a phone booth; but in 1978 the
GOP Convention drew nearly 9,000 delegates and alternates and 1,300
guests to nominate a candidate for the U.S. Senate. In that spacious phone
booth 42-year-old Richard Obenshain wrested the nomination from three

103

candidates, a far cry from the days when the GOP had to draft a sacrificial goat.

Obenshain's interest in politics traced to the GOP National Convention at Chicago in 1952 where, just graduated from high school, he watched the Taft-Eisenhower contest. A liberal professor at New York University School of Law sparked the young man's interest in running for office. A conservative teacher changed the youth's views from moderate Eisenhowerism to pure Goldwater. Obenshain lost a close race for the House of Representatives in Richmond and then another for Virginia Attorney General; but in 1972, taking the chairmanship of the Virginia GOP, Obenshain vowed to make it a "comfortable new home" for conservative Democrats fleeing the liberal takeover of their own party. He reconstructed the Republican Party in his own image.

The Republican Convention in 1978 drew national television coverage through the violet-eyed presence of Elizabeth Taylor, actress-wife of candidate John W. Warner, a former Secretary of the Navy. Cameramen buzzed at her face like bees at a day lily. The idea of running for the Senate had occured to Warner while he was campaigning for Gerald Ford in October 1976 and Senator William Scott announced his intention not to seek re-election. There had been "a question mark about Elizabeth," Warner told a reporter. "I had married her for solely personal reasons with no political thought in mind and there was some speculation the state would not accept her."

In receptions in the state's 10 congressional districts the Warners raised $250,000 for the GOP. Women, more than men, wished to see Elizabeth Taylor, a survivor who had emerged from ordeals—marriages, illnesses, career crises—that would have cowed most women. They came to see if her eyes were really violet and to look for glimpses of the pig-tailed girl in "National Velvet," and for the sheer spectacle of a raven-haired Hollywood celebrity arriving for a political coffee, stepping out of a limousine like an ordinary hausfrau in the broad light of day onto a quiet street between close-clipped lawns in Newport News. Suburbia suddenly became a stage set.

Warner made a dramatic charge in the convention. In the midst of the fifth ballot, the vast throng became aware that Warner, conspicuous in shirt sleeves and wide red-and-blue suspenders, standing on a table in the second tier, his right fist balled, was pumping his arm in a huge semi-circle as he led his supporters in a chant: "GO! . . . GO!"

Former Governor Linwood Holton withdrew on the fourth ballot. On the way to the rostrum he and his family happened to meet Obenshain. Holton shook his hand, the girls kissed him on the cheek, and they climbed the steps to the platform to concede—as much or more a family in defeat as in victory. With a flourish, Holton told the convention: "Fellow Republicans! . . . Jinks, Tayloe, Ann, Woody, and Dwight are very happy to join with you in welcoming me to the status of the elder statesman!" On the convention floor a former member of Holton's administration said, "Had Linwood been less a nonpartisan Governor and more a politician, he could have won tonight."

On the fifth ballot State Senator Nathan Miller of Staunton withdrew from the race and on the sixth ballot Obenshain won. At high points in his acceptance speech, the crowd screamed and waved Obenshain placards —each bearing a huge single O—so that the convention floor looked like a proud, spreading peacock's tail. Obenshain's image had undergone a remarkable transformation in the eyes of many Republicans. Before the nomination he had been portrayed often as highly vulnerable in being "too far to the right." But a deepening trend to conservatism in the electorate and Obenshain's steady march to victory now made him appear to have been the ideal candidate all along.

*   *   *   *

Delegates to the Democratic Convention, a week later on June 9-10 in Williamsburg, found a field of eight candidates. Front-runner Andrew Miller, an unusually able and active Attorney General, had defeated Obenshain for that post in 1969 and lost to Howell in the 1977 Democratic primary for Governor.

If the Republicans had Elizabeth Taylor, the Democrats in William and Mary Hall had a new political force in 300 born-again Christians led by G. Conoly Phillips, a Norfolk councilman and automobile dealer. Their presence prompted a good many good-humored jibes. Seeing Phillips walking onto the floor, one delegate confided to another, "God is his alternate." They looked, en masse, not so much like zealots as comfortably solid members of the average Baptist or Methodist congregation—those who come to church year-round, not just at Christmas or Easter. But their political miracle fizzled. Miller won on the third ballot.

A poignant moment occurred in the hall when Miller arose to accept the nomination. He held out his right hand toward his keen-eyed mother and straight-backed, rosy-faced father sitting in the gallery and said,

"They fought the good fight in politics!" During the delegates' prolonged standing ovation, Colonel Miller, grasping the gallery railing, struggled to his feet, waved to the applauding Democrats, and blew a kiss to the nominee and his bright-eyed wife, Doris, on the platform.

Leading the liberal, anti-Organization wing of the Democratic Party, the Colonel had lost to the Byrd Organization in state races in 1949 and 1952. For daring to decry shortcomings in state government, he was vilified as a "bird who fouls its own nest." But even in defeat on the sidelines, the fires never died. Once, sitting ramrod-straight in an audience listening to an academic conservative condemning the youth of the 1960s, the Colonel bore the tirade a while, then boomed, "Shame! Shame!"

Andrew Miller, consoling the seven losers about the uncertainties of politics, to which, he said, he could testify, set out after the nomination to try to unify a party that had been divided a decade. During the next two months, Obenshain, too, was healing convention wounds. His managers felt his campaign seemed on the upswing. Then came the crash.

On August 2 Obenshain died with two others when the twin-engine plane bringing him from a campaign appearance in Winchester crashed and burned near Chesterfield County Airport. Under the candidate's body, an aide reported, was found an opened book, a complex economics text that Obenshain had been reading even in the midst of a whirlwind campaign.

He secured in Republicans' affections the place that J. Sargeant Reynolds filled with the Democrats. For many, Obenshain had, at first, the reputation of a reserved Goldwater idealogue, a resemblance enhanced by his dark-rimmed glasses. Somewhat shy, really, he wasn't given to backslapping, but a wide, boyish grin showed his delight in seeing a person. In graveside services at the Millcreek Baptist Church in Botetourt County, the Rev. Ray Allen remarked, "Dick never won an election, but any member of his party in Virginia who holds an office owes him a great debt."

Miller, his face darkened with sadness, attended memorial ceremonies for Obenshain in Richmond. Colonel Miller had died August 3 from a stroke suffered shortly after the Democratic convention. The only regret that the old Christian warrior had expressed about his declining health was that he might die "and mess up Andrew's campaign right in the middle." In memorial services for the Colonel in Richmond at Union Theological Seminary, Dr. John Leith said that Miller had "a lover's quarrel" with his state, his nation, and the world.

The face of the campaign changed. Warner, backed vigorously by Governor Dalton, won the nomination from the Republican State Central Committee despite efforts by some GOP right-wingers to recruit another candidate. Throughout the campaign Elizabeth Taylor drew crowds and mishaps. She broke a blood vessel shaking hands in Hampton; swallowed a chicken bone in Big Stone Gap; caught a fleck of metal in her eye in a Richmond pizza parlor; developed bursitis in Galax; appeared in Roanoke with an arm in a sling; suffered laryngitis, weathered mild pneumonia, and showed remarkable recuperative powers. Her part proved vital as Warner won narrowly. He proved to be an energetic U.S. Senator, attentive to constituents' needs. Vice President Bush called him "Mr. Defense" for his work on the Armed Services Committee.

*　　*　　*　　*

In the 1981 race for Governor each candidate's chief problem was with a wing of his own party. Lieutenant Governor Charles S. Robb had to placate Democratic liberals; Attorney General Marshall Coleman had to woo the Republican right. Robb patched together a quilt of blacks, labor, liberals, and moderates with some old-line conservatives who "came home" to the Democratic Party. He was aided in part by the liberals' belated realization that if the Democratic Party, which had been defeated in every major race in 16 years, suffered one more defeat, it might be out of power another 16. Bidding for the right, Coleman repressed some of the instinct for improvisation that had enabled him to shape his own

Coleman　　　　*The Robbs*　　　　*Byrd Jr.*

107

coalition four years previously. Moreover, one setback after another, many of them not of his making, hit Coleman, and Robb won. Coleman's light side, so attractive to aides and so difficult for the media to convey, seldom surfaced during the race.

With reporters after the election, Coleman blamed only himself. "I was the head of the ticket," he told them. "It was my responsibility to win the election, and I didn't do it." Then, mocking his own polls that just before the election had showed him out-distancing Robb, tall, long-jawed Coleman murmured, "I know you think we're still trailing but we've got this overnight tracking sample that shows us ahead."

When he appeared in July, 1982 in the Richmond Coliseum at the Virginia Republican Convention that would nominate a candidate for the U.S. Senate, spectators and reporters clustered around him to shake hands and warm themselves with his humor. Pete Giesen, a GOP leader in the House of Delegates, arrived, a lopsided grin on his face anticipating what Coleman might say. Coleman, who was waiting to introduce members of the General Assembly to the convention, pretended to be at a loss as he scanned his list. "Giesen? Giesen?" said Coleman. "Let's see, are you in the House or the Senate?"

To a newsman who appeared, Coleman remarked, "I didn't see much of you in the campaign. I know, you wished they'd run the *real* Marshall Coleman." A moment later he was telling the cheering, laughing convention: "I will never forget the campaign of 1981. Don't think I haven't tried, but I'll never forget the campaign of 1981!"

*   *   *   *

Startling events marked the start of the 1982 race for a successor to U.S. Senator Harry F. Byrd Jr. who had announced in November "that 18 years is long enough" and that he would not seek re-election. The Democratic leadership, looking for an attractive middle-of-the-road candidate, lit upon Delegate Owen B. Pickett of Virginia Beach, former state party chairman. Kicking off his campaign for the nomination, Pickett twice invoked the name of Harry F. Byrd Sr.

Pickett's gesture to conservatives offended the only black state senator, Richmond's L. Douglas Wilder, already angered by the 1982 General Assembly's failure to pass bills favored by blacks. Wilder threatened to run for the Senate as an independent if Pickett didn't withdraw from the race. The blacks' crucial role in 1981—they cast more than 96 per cent of their 200,000 votes for Robb, who won by a margin of 100,906—

lent force to Wilder's demand. A three-way race with Wilder as an independent would, the Democrats feared, boost Republican Paul S. Trible Jr.'s chances. Pickett withdrew.

Elated Republicans watched half a dozen possible Democratic contenders jostling for position. Party leaders seemed to favor Richard J. Davis, who had been elected Lieutenant Governor on Robb's ticket, but he took himself out of the race. Then, in another surprising twist, three long-time Byrd men—former Governor Mills E. Godwin Jr., Democrat-turned-Republican; former Rep. Watkins M. Abbitt of Appomattox, conservative Democrat, and former Delegate W. Roy Smith of Petersburg, a Democrat-turned-independent—announced that Byrd was willing to reconsider his decision not to seek re-election. Predicting a "better than 50-50 chance" that an outpouring of support would change Byrd's mind about retiring, they launched petitions to put his name on the ballot by the June 8 filing deadline. Though 18 years had seemed "long enough" in December, Byrd seemed tempted to consider his old comrades' pleas for a last hurrah. Still, Byrd, as his father had done, maintained golden silence.

The Byrds always knew how to keep their counsel. At about the time young Harry went to the U.S. Senate, Virginia reporter Don Hill began covering that body. Older hands advised him to greet key senators with the question: "What do you hear?" The approach worked splendidly, inspiring geysers of information, until Hill popped into Byrd's office and inquired, "What do you hear?" And Byrd shot back, "About what?"

The Republicans' glee turned to gloom as Byrd brooded in silence over what to do. Abruptly their prospects had become as bleak as those of the Democrats; but Trible declined, politely but firmly, to get out of the race, and Democrat Davis, scenting a possible three-way fray that would divide the conservatives, intimated he might accept a draft.

How many times Virginians had waited out the Byrds, father and son! How many times Republican conventions had pondered whether to nominate candidates to oppose them. This time the two parties met on the same day, Democrats in Roanoke, Republicans in Richmond, each party with an ear to Byrd's home in Winchester. He would not disclose his decision until after both conventions had adjourned, but a feeling was growing that Byrd would not run.

The Byrds were always astute readers of public opinion. Now the state's newspapers, usually their supporters, urged the Senator to stick by his retirement. The word "integrity" was being heard. Byrd's

Trible   *Wilder*   *Davis*

Republican friends kept excusing themselves from the convention to call Winchester and remind him earnestly that a Byrd never went back on his word. Even liberal Democrats who had never voted for a Byrd felt twinges of regret that their old foe might not act in character.

As conjecture heightened over whether he would run, some advisers figured that although he might well win a three-way race, he scarcely could hope to win a majority of the votes as he had done in 1970 in running as an independent and defeating Republican Ray Garland and Democrat George Rawlings. The Republicans had won a string of victories since that time and the Democrats had pulled themselves together in 1981.

Byrd didn't want to win his last race by a plurality. A campaign would divide old allies and probably play havoc with both parties. Already in anguish were old friends whose abiding rule had been that they would always be for Harry Byrd, but who found themselves pledged to Trible because Byrd had announced in December that he wouldn't run.

In Richmond the attitude in the Republican Convention was not so much bitter as it was calm and determined. It signified a kind of coming of age of the Republican Party as it went about nominating Trible. Ordinarily, having been nominated, a candidate makes a grand exit and goes to some retreat to rest. Trible came down to mingle with departing delegates, sign autographs, pose for pictures, and promise to "keep in touch." The last scene in the nearly empty Coliseum was Trible shaking hands with the members of the band.

In Roanoke the Democrats nominated Davis. As a businessman and former mayor of Portsmouth, he knew the problems of inner cities. If he lagged behind Trible in collecting campaign funds, Davis's recent campaign with Robb gave him a slight edge in the polls as the race began. It was as if a masterly handicapper had arranged events to assure as tight a race as possible.

Byrd declined to run again for auld ang syne. For the first time in this century, ever since Richard Evelyn Byrd, Old Harry's father, was Speaker of the House of Delegates, Virginia was without a Byrd in a high place in its government. It also marked the first time in Virginia that a black office-holder had turned one party in its tracks and very nearly brought an upheaval in the other. Some Democrats felt resentment at the way Wilder jerked around the party, but then the Richmond Senator's view was that his race had been jerked around, even as it was delivering solid blocs of votes to one and another candidate for Governor.

When Congress abolished the poll tax in federal elections in 1965 and the U.S. Supreme Court struck it from state elections, politicians had to consider the views of blacks. They became a part of James Madison's equation of government in which competing special interests achieve a balancing effect for the common good. In Virginia, trying power newly bestowed on them, blacks had a vital effect in nearly every state-wide election. In 1965 they helped elect Mills Godwin Governor over Republican Linwood Holton despite Godwin's espousal of Massive Resistance in the 1950s. Then in 1969 enough blacks supported Holton to assure his election as Governor against Democrat William C. Battle.

To issue statistics on the numbers of blacks appointed to jobs and boards no longer sufficed. What Wilder sought was consideration of legislation that affected the entire community of blacks.

In a race marked by bitter exchanges and record expenditures, Trible defeated Davis. Costs of two races for the House of Representatives in 1982 exceeded those of gubernatorial campaigns of the 1950s. Harry Byrd Jr. went back to Winchester in much the mood he had arrived in Washington—at odds with a President who could not grasp the importance of cutting budget deficits.

*   *   *   *

Virginia lost the services of two public figures, those of House Speaker John Warren Cooke through his retirement and former Governor Colgate W. Darden Jr. by his death.

The son of Confederate veteran Giles B. Cooke who rode from Appomattox with Robert E. Lee, John Warren Cooke rose through the conservative Democratic Organization, but he exercised power in a fair, enlightened fashion. Like his father, who after the war became a clergyman and founded a school for black children in Petersburg, John Warren was aware of the underdog. He worked a quiet revolution by appointing blacks, women, liberals, and Republicans to major committees in the House of Delegates. He brought them into the House's major committees, out of the cold from committees that never met.

"They had constituencies to represent," Cooke said. "Those constituencies had to be heard." When Cooke retired in 1979 after 36 years in the House and 12 as its Speaker, Republican Ray Garland was moved almost to tears at the prospect of legislative life without the square, massive Cooke looking dark-eyed and impartial on the 100 members. Delegate Mary Marshall recalled the penetrating stare the Speaker directed at any lobbyist who chanced to encroach onto the floor during a session.

Lobbyists' activities intensified to the point that Lynchburg State Senator Elliott Schewel revived William Rawlings' efforts to have the General Assembly tighten its code of ethics. After three years of wrangling, the State Senate of 1982 strengthened rules requiring members to disclose business interests and adopted a reform offered by Majority Leader Hunter Andrews and Norfolk Senator Stanley Walker providing an ethics committee of five non-legislators. The Senate failed again to prohibit legislators from representing paying clients before the state's regulatory boards, and the House of Delegates did nothing at all. To put Virginia gentlemen under anything but their own oath was an affront, some legislators held. On the one hand they contended that vigilant newspapers were a sufficient safeguard against conflicts of interest and on the other that newspapers had blown the issue out of proportion. But the issue would not go away.

An exponent of the state's integrity, former Governor Darden was his active, committed self to the end despite pain from a World War I injury and high blood pressure. Though warned not to subject himself to stress, Darden was always agreeing to one last act of service. Thus, after pondering a week, he nominated Robb for Governor on May 30, 1981. "If I had failed to do it," he told a reporter, "and that boy had lost, I'd have been haunted by it." Ten days later Darden died.

Darden's readiness to take the unpopular side of an issue, if he judged it correct, made what he said count as much as what he did. That sense

Boothe   *F. P. Miller*   *Cooke*

of a tough, far-seeing mind at work on public issues heartened an entire state and especially its dissenters. It gave others the courage to speak out. In 1949 when Delegate Armistead Boothe of Alexandria was sponsoring bills to abolish segregation on buses, streetcars, and trains, he sat near Darden on a public platform. Darden, then president of the University of Virginia, called to Boothe and said, casually, that if Boothe cared to subpoena him, he'd be glad to testify for the bills.

In his inaugural speech Robb commented that Darden's willingness to nominate him "was a gracious gesture whose importance to me is exceeded only by the immense influence he had upon me in the time I was privileged to have his friendship and counsel." Much of their talk in Norfolk at Darden's office overlooking the Elizabeth River dealt with the importance of education to Virginians. Robb set better education as his first priority in announcing his candidacy; and his first budget as Governor provided a raise in teacher salaries.

Darden's career-long crusade was to improve public education. After serving as Governor and university president he worked eight years as a member of the State Board of Education and wrote the constitutional amendment, ratified with other changes in 1970, guaranteeing an education of high quality for every child in Virginia. It was another step, really, in Thomas Jefferson's struggle for a system of public education.

Legislators have temporized with the mandate for quality; but the General Assembly's greatest act would be to provide funds to give Virginia's children the best education in the United States. Too often pupils move from grade to grade without knowing even how to read. Lacking that key to survival in our society, compounding failures, they finally drop out of school onto the streets and into crime.

Virginians are always turning, understandably, to Jefferson for guidance. His mind is casting forever ahead of us. Writing to John Adams in their old age, Jefferson recalled the failure of the General Assembly to adopt his ambitious bill for the more general diffusion of knowledge in educating the people.

"I have great hope," Jefferson wrote, "that some patriotic spirit will . . . call it up and make it the keystone of the arch of our government."

Nothing would assure as bright a future if patriotic spirits would call it up and make it the keystone of the arch of our government today. Virginia's children deserve it.

Thomas Jefferson, by Jean Antoine Houdon

A VIRGINIA GALLERY

PHOTOGRAPHS: Gunston Hall, p. 119, *Taylor Lewis Jr.;* Rotunda, p. 123, *Robert Llewellyn;* The Manse, p. 125, *Woodrow Wilson Foundation;* Mountain Sunset, p. 127, and Powell Valley Barn, p. 129, *William Portlock Jr.;* St. Paul's Church, p. 143, *Betsy Batten;* Swans at Back Bay, p. 147, *Chris Hartman;* all others, courtesy *Virginia State Travel Service.*

THE FARMER OF MOUNT VERNON

Yoked with a desire to stay "under my own vine and fig tree" at Mount Vernon was a sense of duty that drove George Washington to serve his country. He was that rarity, the indispensable man.

The army, a seasonal thing with three-month enlistments, dwindled at times to 1,500 men. The new-founded Congress often seemed a windy forensic society, and the infant 13 states as frail and wavering as rustling reeds along a Tidewater creek. The grand constant, the sustaining force on the road to Yorktown, was George Washington's character.

He knew, going into it, what he faced. In June, 1775, shortly after the Continental Congress had elected him commander-in-chief, Washington told Patrick Henry, "Remember, Mr. Henry, what I now tell you; from the day I enter upon the command of the American armies, I date my fall, and the ruin of my reputation." When the ragtag army was encamped at Harlem Heights, he wrote his cousin Lund at Mount Vernon: "If I were to wish the bitterest curse to an enemy on this side of the grave, I should put him in my stead with my feelings." After the march to Valley Forge through sleet and snow, Washington wrote: "You might have tracked the army by the blood of their feet."

Yet his troops never heard from their commander's mouth, a severe straight line, as if he were tasting bad medicine, a word of dispair. Time after time in desperate situations, Washington would be in the midst of the troops, as if dropped from the clouds, an apparition in buff and blue on a huge white horse, rallying them, oblivious himself to the hail of musket balls. His aim was simply to maintain at least a semblance of an army. Then, when the French intervened and Admiral De Grasse's fleet bottled up British General Cornwallis in Yorktown, George Washington put it all together and won the last battle and the war.

His country called again and he accepted the presidency. After one term he thought he had done enough, but, as Jefferson pleaded: "The confidence of the whole nation is centered in you. Your being at the helm will be more than an answer to every argument which can be used to alarm and lead the people into violence and secession. North and South will hang together if they have you to hang on."

Finally, the farmer went home.

GEORGE MASON'S LEGACY

His country's business was always dragging George Mason from Gunston Hall, his "elegant little mansion." When George Washington took command of the Revolutionary army, Mason replaced him in the Virginia Convention in Williamsburg. "I was never in so disagreeable a situation and almost dispaired of a cause which I saw so ill conducted," Mason wrote Washington. "Mere vexation and disgust threw me into such an ill state of health . . . . I was sometimes near fainting in the house."

Yet, Mason was ready with the right words at the crucial moment, as when he listed guarantees for individual liberties in the Virginia Declaration of Rights. Its influence on Jefferson's Declaration of Independence is evident in Mason's first article: "All Men are born equally free and independent" with inherent natural rights that include "the Enjoyment of Life and Liberty, with the means of acquiring and possessing Property and pursueing and obtaining Happiness and Safety."

On a principle, the portly gray-eyed man could be an unmovable wedge. In 1787 when the Philadelphia Convention, framing the Federal Constitution, failed to abolish slave trade or adopt a bill of rights, Mason refused to sign the document. In the Virginia Convention, called a year later in Richmond to ratify the Constitution, an aged, ill Mason directed his final public words against the "diabolical" slave trade.

The tension throughout Mason's life, an intensely private person pulled again and again into public affairs, is reflected in his will where he urges his sons "to prefer the happiness of independence & a private Station to the troubles and Vexations of Public Business . . ."

But, the patriot spirit rising in him, he adds: "but if either their own inclination or the Necessity of the times shou'd engage them in Public Affairs, I charge them on a Father's blessing, never to let the motives of private interest or ambition to induce them to betray, nor the terrors of Poverty and disgrace, for the fear of danger or of death deter them from Asserting the Liberty of their Country, and endeavoring to transmit to their posterity those Sacred rights to which themselves were born."

Once George Washington asked: "Mr. Mason, what services in the power of the people can I bestow on you?" And Mason replied: "Your services as President of the United States, Mr. Washington."

THE MIND AT MONTICELLO

No home bespeaks the builder more clearly than does Monticello. Like its creator, it is forever disclosing another facet. Other planters built homes on rivers near wharfs; Jefferson set his on a mountain and terraced and planted the mountain until it seemed a hanging basket of trees and gardens. Monticello contains 35 rooms, but to minimize the mass, Jefferson hid dependencies below terraces, set back a half story, and lengthened windows to cover a story and a half. Labor-saving gadgets greet one at every turn.

"I don't see how he could do and be so many things," President Truman murmured, on a visit there. Besides genius, Jefferson had a robust body, which he respected and exercised. He did things when he thought of them; he had good taste, an insatiable curiosity—"I am interested in every sprig of grass that grows," he wrote his daughter Martha—faith in his countrymen, and an optimistic outlook. "My temperament is sanguine," he wrote John Adams. "I steer my bark with Hope in the head, leaving fear astern. My hopes, indeed, sometimes fail; but not oftener than the foreboding of the gloomy."

While Washington was fighting a revolution, Jefferson was writing one, revising all Virginia laws. "Our Revolution," he wrote, "presented us an album on which we were free to write what we pleased." It was time for fixing every essential right on a legal basis because, he reasoned, after the war the people would be forgotten and their rights disregarded and would forget themselves in making money.

By far the most important bill, he declared, was one to establish a public school system "for diffusion of knowledge among the people." No other sure foundation could be devised for preserving freedom and happiness. "Preach, my dear sir," he wrote George Wythe, "a crusade against ignorance, establish and improve the law for educating the common people. Let our countrymen know . . . that the tax which will be paid for this purpose is not more than the thousandth part of what will be paid to kings, priests, and nobles who will rise up among us if we leave the people in ignorance."

Had Virginians heeded Jefferson, an educated electorate could have resisted secession. Without Virginia, the other Southern states wouldn't have warred for long.

A HYMN TO REASON

Thomas Jefferson founded the University of Virginia as "the last act of usefulness I can render." He struggled five years to coax appropriations through the General Assembly, designed an academic village around the Lawn with the Rotunda as the centerpiece, devised the curriculum, supervised the choosing of the faculty, shaped the board of visitors, and rode from Monticello nearly every day to check the construction. On days when bad weather kept him at Monticello, he peered through a telescope to follow the progress of his University, abuilding far below. Today a visitor, from a walkway under Monticello's white dome, can look far down the mountain to the Rotunda's white dome framed through an opening in the trees. It is as if the spectator peering through that opening, is gazing backward through time.

In 1976 the University restored the Rotunda's interior to Jefferson's design, including the huge room under the dome, frequently termed "the most beautiful room in America." A visitor walks up a narrow, winding stairway and pops gopher-like into the towering light-filled room and feels a sudden exhilaration, as if entering a larger, sunnier world where things are in exquisite proportion. To begin, there is the sheer vastness of the great hemisphere that measures 77 feet across and 51 feet in height from the pine flooring to the huge skylight centered in the dome. Two balconies, supported by a double row of twin columns, 40 columns in all, rim the room. Recessed behind the 20 pairs of columns are back-to-back bookcases.

The great room—soaring dome, columns, walls—is painted white. The skylight high overhead, offering glimpses of blue skies and drifting white clouds by day and stars by night, enhances a sense of airiness. When shafts of sunlight slant through the opening in the dome and strike the trunks of the white columns and splash in a golden patch on the warm wood floor, the visitor feels he has come upon an opening in a forest. By night, light beams through the windows rimming the dome and pours upward through the skylight, a beacon of knowledge.

The building is a series of revelations with the dome room outdoing them all. The soft white walls and columns, the great expanse, the soaring dome and spherical shape convey coolness, serenity, and rationality. It is Jefferson's hymn to reason.

THE MAN FROM THE MANSE

In Staunton is the Manse where Woodrow Wilson was born and lived until he was eight months old. Then his father, a Presbyterian minister, accepted an invitation to a church in Georgia. Both Georgia and North Carolina, where Wilson attended Davidson College, claim him, but during the 1912 presidential campaign, he declared: "I am a Virginian." Reading and writing American history strengthened his resolve to align himself with the Virginians of the American Revolution. With his plan for the League of Nations, Wilson displayed statecraft not seen since Madison led in drafting the U.S. Constitution; his way with words is reminiscent of Jefferson's; his adherence to principle recalls staunch George Mason's stick-to-it-tiveness.

At any rate if Wilson's stay in the Manse was brief, the foundation has collected enough memorabilia to make it seem that he never left. To understand the Christian soldier, one should visit the Manse and hear the chimes from his father's church a block away and see the piano where the family gathered to sing hymns and look at the cradle that rocked somebody who rocked the world for a time with a dream of peace.

When Wilson returned to Staunton for a birthday party in December, 1912, his remarks at the townspeople's banquet demonstrated his feel for metaphor and a politician's knack to weave, while gazing into well-fed faces, a theme: "Men believe now that sooner or later their wrongs are going to be righted, and that a time is going to dawn when justice will be the average and useful thing in the administration of human affairs.

"You may imagine the pleasure, therefore, that it gives me to look back to the place where these standards cannot be questioned, for these standards were first established, so far as this side of the water is concerned, in Virginia. And no Virginian can stand up and look the history of Virginia in the face and doubt what the future is going to be. If I have any advantage as a Virginian, it is merely that I have gotten a running start. A man that ties in with communities of this sort began further back and the further back you got your start, the greater the momentum. And all that is needed is momentum. It does not need any cunning tongue. It does not need eloquence. It just needs the kind of serenity which enables you to steer by the stars and not the ground."

HOMECOMING

In late August, when days are mild and bright with a hint of autumn in the air, there always is a homecoming at the Mount Rogers Baptist Church in these golden hills of Southwest Virginia. Decoration Day, it is called, when people gather, some of them from as far away as California, to tidy up the resting places of their ancestors, those who have gone ahead, farther even than California.

Down a lane at the foot of Haw Orchard Mountain hundreds were returning to place flowers in a graveyard so ancient that time and weather have leveled many graves with the earth. In the older portions of the graveyard, fieldstone markers seem mere granite outcroppings from the slant mountainside.

From a distance, the hum of the multitude muted, people of all ages and attire moving about the graveyard, it looked as though a rainbow had shattered in the earth's broad lap.

Children, their mothers chasing them, were flying about the tombstones. Young girls entering the gateway were lifting their hands to their hair for a final pat. Older women, carrying galvanized tin washtubs of flowers, stooped to arrange tiger lillies, painted daisies, gladiolas, bells of Ireland, and dahlias. Their clothes—red, blue, green, orange, yellow, pink—seemed moving flowers. The community might have gathered leisurely for the last trump to go to the other side.

The bell in the white church began to ring. The notes sank quickly in the peace and stillness of the hill country. Few made a move to go inside until a hymn—"Fill my way every day with love"—floated through the open windows.

Visiting preachers took turns at the pulpit while women set dinner outside on shaded trestle tables at the foot of the graveyard. Mothers already were quieting children with wishbones. Giant white clouds, motionless as in a picture puzzle, peeped over the mountains at the scene.

Near a grave a man in a derby talked earnestly to a friend, motioning, it seemed, at the mound at their feet, describing emphatically a cherished someone—loyal, loving, untiring. I eased nearer to catch more of the paragon, just in time to hear the man in the derby saying, "Anyway, we lost him, and he was the best track-dog we ever had."

126

POWELL VALLEY BARN

The gray barn on the hill is as much a natural part of Powell Valley as the snow capping the mountains above it. Scenes like these get in the blood. The people, too, become one with nature. They become attuned to the seasons' slow turnings. Their tall mountains call for tales as tall. A man has to express himself to match the hills. That winter, remember, it was so cold? Word came from the mountains that two hounds had been seen trying to start a rabbit with jump cables.

The mountains, when you get to the top of one, stretch away fold on fold, to the horizon, gray hump-backed whales, browsing. So narrow are the defiles between their flanks that you only see the sun at noon. And then you have to lie on your back, a fellow says, looking you in the eye. Old-timers insist that cattle have to be bred short-legged on one side to stand on the steep hillsides. If, plowing, you fell off one of those hills, you'd fall up, they say. On the other hand, if you're a miner working a coal seam in one of those mountains, it can get so narrow there, you have to come outside to turn over the pick, they swear.

Hard times periodically disperse Southwest Virginia families. A man finds a job in Evansville or Gary and sends for those at home. An entire church congregation, family by family, moves to another state, then sends for the preacher. Carrying Virginia with them. Some Northern industrial centers have more Southwest Virginians than do the towns they left behind. But the exiles come back. On a weekend they light out and travel a thousand miles to rest in the folds of the hills. "This world is not my home, I'm just a passing through/My treasures are laid up somewhere beyond the blue," they sing in Cleveland, thinking of Big Stone Gap. Southwest Virginians who have lived elsewere 10 years or longer often feel that they are on temporary leave from their true home, back in the hills.

A fellow went away to the big city, Dayton or Dee-troit, to work in the ice-box factory. The pay was good, but after a while he went to the foreman and said he was leaving, going home.

"Why?," the foreman asked. "The pay here is better."

The mountaineer said, "Yes, the pay is better here, but the day is better there."

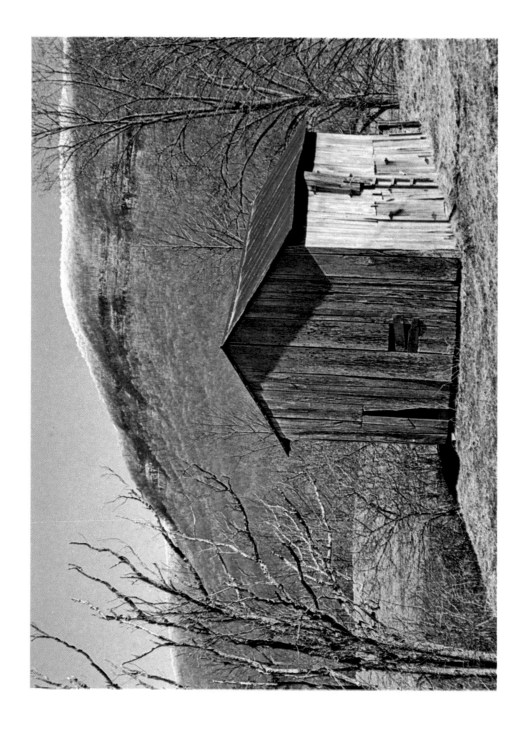

BLUE RIDGE FARM

Let a Virginian speak casually of the Valley of Virginia and odds are he is referring to the Shenandoah Valley, reaching from a point north of Winchester on the Maryland-Virginia line southwest to Buchanan County, but the GREAT Valley extends across the state to Bristol and beyond. Along with the Shenandoah segment, there are the Fincastle Valley from Buchanan to Christiansburg, the Dublin Valley from Christiansburg to Marion, and the Abingdon Valley to the Tennessee line. When a Virginian says he is from the Valley, he opens up a vista.

The hugh trough lies between the Blue Ridge, the backbone down the center of the state, and the Alleghenies to the west of Staunton. Once a vast sea lapped at the Blue Ridge's western slopes. When the hills barely hump their backs above the white morning mists, it seems that the waters have come again.

Squiggling along the Blue Ridge is the 105-mile Skyline Drive. From Hogback Overlook, you can count 11 bends in the Shenandoah River. At Afton, the Skyline Drive changes its name to the Blue Ridge Parkway and winds 217 miles to North Carolina. Sweeping across the Valley floor in a broad swath is Interstate 81 down which industries have poured into the Valley where pioneers trudged. Nearby is old U.S. Route 11, a neighborly road that visits towns.

On the Blue Ridge Parkway the visitor finds a mountain farm snuggled in the green folds of the hills. In late April colleges around Roanoke host a wildflower pilgrimage. Ascending Apple Orchard Mountain, the pilgrims chart spring's progress. In three hours they travel three weeks, from green slopes at the foot, where spring reigns full force, to the chilled brown heights of Sunset Fields where winter still camps. Pressed in memory is a wooded slope strewn with dozens of pink lady slippers, as if someone, dressing in a hurry, had flung satin shoes in all directions.

In the fall Virginians flock to the Valley and marvel at the Blue Ridge's raiment in shades of red, orange, yellow, bronze, and purple, stitched in evergreen. The effect, as with camouflage, is to render a most substantial mountain into a wavery, vari-hued veil that could be parted with the hand. They feel, gazing at the robe of many colors, that they have touched eternity.

THE VOICE IN ST. JOHN'S

Patrick Henry "certainly gave the first impulse to the ball of the Revolution," said Thomas Jefferson. Opposing the British Stamp Act in a speech May 29, 1765 in the House of Burgesses in Williamsburg, Henry cried: "Tarquin and Caesar had each his Brutus, Charles the First his Cromwell, and George the Third—"

"Treason!" shouted Speaker John Robinson and others. Henry, drawing back adroitly, finished his sentence: ". . . may profit by their example. If THIS be treason, make the most of it!" Some historians insist Henry apologized by concluding: "And George the Third, may he never have either!"

When Henry spoke, people forgot to make notes. Even court clerks laid down their pens. His speeches, historian Joseph Roberts notes, have had to be reconstructed from their foundations like the dwellings in Colonial Williamsburg. Henry gave the ball another powerful thrust on March 23, 1775. Delegates to the Second Virginia Convention assembled at St. John's Church, Richmond's largest building. Urging them to put Virginia in a state of defense, Henry defined the choice: "Is life so dear or peace so sweet, as to be purchased at the price of chains or slavery? Forbid it, Almighty God! I know not what course others may take but as for me, give me liberty or give me death!"

Henry suspected all government, even the one he helped found. At the convention meeting June 2, 1788 in Richmond, he opposed Virginia's ratifying the Constitution. The document, he cried, was said to have beautiful features, "but when I come to examine those features, Sir, they appear to me horribly frightful. Among other deformities it has an awful squinting—it squints toward monachy. . . ." It needed, he and Mason harped, a bill of rights. Madison later saw to that.

Henry had a high brow, deep-socketed blue eyes, and a wide mouth that stretched to his long jaws' outermost edges. His lips dipped at the center and turned down at the ends, and the orator's mouth, when closed, looked like the silhouette of a Hanover turkey buzzard in flight. A casual remark from Henry about the weather as he entered a tavern was enough, a contemporary said, to stop conversation and rivet attention. He could walk out on a hillside and make himself heard to people working in a field a half mile away. On occasion, his voice carried around the world.

JOHN MARSHALL'S COURT

Because John Marshall's beloved wife, Polly, was an invalid, he often went to market in Richmond's Shockoe Bottom and returned, a rangy, carelessly dressed figure laden with turnips and fowles, entering the square brick house at Tenth and Marshall Streets. A newcomer to Richmond met Marshal coming home from market and, taking him for a delivery-man, asked him to carry a turkey and gave him a tip. When the newcomer learned his porter's name, he tried to apologize. "Oh, we were going the same way," Marshall said, smiling—and kept the tip.

The fourth and great Chief Justice, Marshall made the U.S. Supreme Court supreme. In *Marbury v. Madison* in 1803 his opinion affirmed the Court's authority to review the constitutionality of acts of Congress: "It is a proposition too plan to be contested . . . there is no middle ground . . . The Constitution is superior to any ordinary act of the legislature."

Justices of our day, criticized as usurping legislative authority, aren't a patch on John Marshall's robe. Marshall's foes said that when he couldn't find a precedent for what was too plain to be contested, he set one. Fast as Jefferson appointed members to the Court, Marshall charmed them to his own way of thinking. Quick-witted, winsome, he could see straight to the heart of a case or a jest. In a Philadelphia club a friend challenged Marshall to use the word "paradox" in verse. Spying Kentuckians drinking corn liquor at the bar, Marshall responded:

In the bluegrass region of Kentucky, a paradox was born,
The corn was full of kernels, and the colonels full of corn.

His portrait shows an arresting face: long-drawn, square-chinned, with deep-set dark and glowing eyes and firm, straight mouth. Of thorough, quick resolve, he could relax and enjoy good companionship, as he did reading aloud with Polly, taking her out of town to escape the noise of the Fourth of July, and writing her, when apart, tender notes, love letters of a life-time. He also enjoyed camaraderie at the Barbecue Club on Parson John Buchanan's farm, swapping yarns and tossing quoits or horseshoes. As you pass 1000 West Clay Street, know that here the Chief Justice threw horseshoes and got on his knees to measure a close one with a straw.

A PALACE REFURBISHED

Discovery of documents itemizing contents of the Governor's Palace moved Colonial Williamsburg to spend $1 million refurbishing it in 1981.

Now, more than ever, it is a palace. The entrance hall, formerly of dark wood dispensing gloom, is ablaze with 600 muskets, swords, and pistols. A pinwheel of polished muskets adorns the ceiling. Crossed swords, gleaming, lattice a wall. An oval of pistols with silver barrels and bronze butts borders a delicately tinted coat of arms, the pistols the petals in a martial flower. The weaponry, a woven steel fabric, was added to the walls as a reminder of Britain's might when it was already waning in the Colony.

From that silent, glittering arsenal, a visitor steps into the ballroom, formerly a muted green, now an intense blue reminiscent of a cloudless sky shortly past noon on a hot summer's day. Such changes didn't win universal acclaim, many Virginians believing that in anything touching Virginia the best change is no change. "I authorized the dismantling of some of the most beautiful rooms in America," said Carlisle Humelsine, Colonial Williamsburg's board chairman. "Many of my friends ask, 'Why didn't you leave well enough alone at the Palace?' "

From the start in 1926 Colonial Williamsburg has been committed to authenticity in restoring the 18th century town. Advances in scholarship had dictated changes to depict life as it was in the 15 years before the American Revolution during the reigns of jolly Lord Botetourt and dour Lord Dunmore. In scholarship, like something out of "Alice in Wonderland," the further you get from a subject, the clearer it becomes.

English Georgian in design and Renaissance in spirit, the Palace of 61 rooms and 10 acres of gardens was the residence of seven Royal Governors and Virginia's first two elected Governors, Patrick Henry and Thomas Jefferson. It remained the Commonwealth's executive headquarters until the capital moved to Richmond in 1781. Three days before Christmas following the victory over the British at Yorktown, the Palace, while still serving as a military hospital, burned to the ground. Colonial Williamsburg rebuilt it from scratch.

Women, especially, bask in Williamsburg's well-ordered world. It's their idea of paradise, with everything an antique and in place.

ALL FOR LIBERTY

Directing an American battery's bombardment of British forces in Yorktown on October 10, 1781, General Lafayette asked the advice of General Thomas Nelson, Virginia's war-time Governor who also commanded the state militia during the siege. Nelson, a Yorktown resident, pointed to his own house.

"There, to that house," he said. "There you will be most certain to find Lord Cornwallis and the British headquarters. Never spare a particle of my property so long as it affords a shelter to the enemies of my country."

As the cannonading began, Nelson turned and rode away. The portly Governor did not cut an heroic figure, but no finer patriot existed. His Georgian house, a massive brick structure with stone trim facing Yorktown's Main Street, still bears scars of the bombardment, badges of honor.

When the Governor's aides urged him to stay in Richmond, he replied that he should be in the field where the "wants of the Army which are many, and which require the most instant attention, are here represented to me on the spot."

His self sacrifice at the Yorktown siege typified his service as a legislator. When the House of Delegates considered in 1777 a bill authorizing Virginians to use depreciated paper currency in paying debts to British merchants, Nelson contended that would be a breach of contract and show ingratitude to many British creditors who could be regarded as benefactors of Virginians. "I hope the bill will be rejected," Nelson said, "but whatever its fate, I will pay my debts like an honest man."

During the war he paid for supplies for the army. He paid dearly with his health, too. Virginia's failure after the war to repay funds he had advanced for loan drives heightened his difficulties in supporting a large family and in struggling to pay his own pre-war debts to British merchants. When Nelson died at 50, his doctor noted "that the exquisite tortures of the mind were the disease that destroyed his body."

Newspapers announcing his death were edged in black. "There is but one to whom his country (Virginia) is more indebted," one stated. In the graveyard of Grace Church an inscription on Nelson's tomb reads: *He Gave All for Liberty*. His is one of eight likenesses in bronze surrounding the equestrian statue of George Washington in Capitol Square in Richmond.

THE HOME OF THE LEES

Thomas Lee, a Burgess who became President of His Majesty's Council, built Stratford Hall to last. Brick walls two feet thick stand on the ground, as if the house grew there, in Westmoreland County, a bulwark against Indians, wars, and time itself. Splendidly symmetrical, it forms an H, as if to signify the first letter in House on an ABC block. Two wings, 60 feet by 30 feet, form uprights of the H; the central hall, 30 feet by 30 feet, is the cross bar. The great hall opens from the second story onto stairs to the lawn.

Down the fan-shaped steps came four generations of public servants, including 12 Burgesses, four Governors. Of Thomas Lee's sons, Richard Henry and Francis Lightfoot signed the Declaration of Independence, Arthur and William became the new nation's diplomats, and Thomas Ludwell labored in the House of Burgesses. "A band of brothers," John Adams exulted, "intrepid and unchangeable, who like the Greeks of Thermopylae stood in the gap, in the defence of their country . . ."

A sister, Hannah, was as resolute as the brothers. After her husband died, Hannah managed the estate and, finding that women could not vote, she protested to brother Richard Henry. In a long letter in which he promised to try to change things, he wrote: "Perhaps 'twas thought rather out of character for women to press into . . . tumultuous assemblages of men where the . . . choosing representatives is conducted . . ." To deny women the right to vote was taxation without representation, Hannah retorted, the point Americans were contesting with the British.

Hannah fell in love with Dr. Richard Hall, and they joined the Baptist Church. Baptist marriage ceremonies were illegal, and, moreover, her husband's will specified that she lose the estate if she remarried. Undaunted, the couple lived happily with their two children without wedding bonds but with the community's acceptance. Hannah declared her independence.

Robert E. Lee was born at Stratford. It has the cradle that rocked him, and, in a small fireplace in the nursery, an iron fireback depicting two chubby cherubs that fascinated him. Plagued by debts, the family had to move to Alexandria, but when time came for the carriage to leave Stratford, Robert, not quite 4, was missing. They found him at the fireback, saying goodbye to the cherubs.

A SHOT IN THE CRAW

Amid downtown Norfolk's modern bank buildings and civic center is Old St. Paul's green lawn and tilted tombstones in deep shade. Magnolias cloak the old brick church. In its south wall is a cannonball lobbed there January 1, 1776 by Lord Dunmore, Virginia's last royal governor.

The church, built in 1739, is the only pre-revolutionary building left standing after the torch was put to the town, first by the British and then by Colonial troops. No other city bore as much as Norfolk in the American Revolution. In late February 1776 only charred ruins remained.

The agony began at 3 o'clock on a cold New Year's afternoon. Dunmore, who had fled the Colonial Capitol at Williamsburg, had four ships fire broadsides that punched holes in buildings. Redcoat sorties ashore destroyed 19 homes. When the British returned to their ships, Colonial troops turned to Norfolk's destruction partly because of its many Scottish merchants. In three days of burning and pillaging, the patriots destroyed 863 buildings. Then, to prevent the town's ever serving as a British base, the Virginia Convention in February ordered the remaining 416 houses destroyed. Norfolk, which had rivaled the port of New York, was no more.

A lottery raised funds to rebuild and roof St. Paur's broken walls. In 1848, digging in the ground, Norfolkians found a cannonball that had left a dent in the south wall. They morticed the ball into place. Just a few inches to the east, and it would have missed and Norfolk would have lost an heirloom.

Fire and flood visited the city. Yellow fever scourged it four times. Only a frost in 1855 broke the pestilence that took 2,000 lives. Jefferson's embargo of 1907 and the British Blockade in 1812 crippled the port. The General Assembly chose to build canals in piedmont instead of railroads to the sea. "Beast" Butler occupied Norfolk during the Civil War. Slums had to be cleared after World War II with the nation's first urban renewal fund. "It's just been one thing after another, hasn't it?" Governor Colgate Darden Jr. once sighed. Yet Norfolk always comes back stronger. And there's a cannonball in its craw to remind it that it always can.

In spring, when earth is warming, crowds gather for lunch in the churchyard—black and white, old and young—and listen to hard rock, soft soul, or hot jazz and a youth, his back to a tombstone, reads poetry to the quick and the dead.

CHINCOTEAGUE'S MARSHES

A visitor, leaving Route 13 and following a causeway to Chincoteague, crosses marshes of lush green, threaded by blue waters, flecked with snowy egrets and red-winged blackbirds sporting red and yellow chevrons. Chincoteague appears, white and pastel cottages, roofs slanted like artists' easels, white under the sun between green marsh and blue sky.

Chincoteague is one of a dozen barrier islands off Eastern Shore, a narrow, 70-mile peninsula washed on one side by the Chesapeake Bay, on the other by the Atlantic, and laced with thousands of creeks. You are ever aware of the water. During an oyster roast in late fall near Cape Charles, the guests quieted toward sundown and turned to watch the blazing red ball sinking to the Bay's western rim. It touched the edge, poised a moment, and dropped from sight all at once, abruptly as a nickle slipped into a slot machine. The guests applauded. The precipitate leave-taking left the waters a lovely, darkening lavender.

The Shore has persons who rival the sun. At a lane's end off Route 13, is the site of the estate of Arlington. In the family graveyard lies John Custis IV who died, the tombstone says: "Aged 71 years/and yet liv'd but Seven Years which/was the span of time He kept a Batchelers/ house at Arlington on the Eastern Shore/of Virginia."

Colonel Custis and his wife Frances, daughter of Daniel Parke, governor of Leeward Islands, were strong-willed, hot-tempered, forever quarreling. At last they decided to speak only through a slave Pompey. The Colonel invited his wife for a carriage drive; but after riding a short distance across the hard-packed sand, he drove the horse into the Bay.

"Where are you going, Colonel Custis?" she asked.

"To hell, madam!" he retorted.

"Drive on," she said, "any place is better than Arlington!"

He turned to shore. "Madam," he said, "I believe you would as lief meet the Devil himself if I should drive to hell."

"Quite true, Sir," she said. "I know you so well I would not be afraid to go anywhere you would go."

The boy and girl, walking hand in hand through Chincoteague's green marshes, know better.

SWANS IN BACK BAY

Early on a January morning in the Back Bay Wildlife Refuge near Virginia Beach 200 whistling swans nestled on the water, their heads tucked under their wings against the cold. The just risen sun, a burning bon fire on the horizon, shone on the swans, turning them into hummocks of glistening, pink-tinted snow.

A stick cracked. Their heads jerked up in unison, slim straight palings of a white picket fence against the deep blue water. They took off, running on the water with their huge webbed feet, rising, a snowfall reversed, stroking the air with their great wings, heads and neck stretched arrow-straight. The whistle-like blasts from the long windpipes split the air. On a still day you can hear them a mile away, faintly, as of some baying hounds yelping on a heavenly trace.

From sunrise to sunset during fall, winter, and early spring, visitors may watch, for free, the magnificent spectacle of a swan easing in for a landing, its outspread wings spanning six feet, the sun shining through translucent lower wing linings. Just before it touches down, the great bird sets back those wings like nylon chutes and pushes out gawky black webbed feet that act as buoys, and settles on the water so softly not a feather is mussed. It furls its wings as gracefully as a ballerina taking a bow for a flawless performance.

In the peak of the season, mid-December, 10,000 swans populate the marshes of Back Bay, a great white fleet sailing majestically in open stretches or anchoring in the coves. As winter wanes, they become restless, gabbing away about the yearning to get going, talking it over among themselves. By early March they have all departed for their summer home in the Arctic. Like the ice floes they resemble, they begin to disappear when the weather turns balmy.

Once swans were hunted almost to extinction. Now, after being protected 60 years, they number 100,000. Swans mate for life, produce two or three young each year. When one adult of a pair dies, thenceforth the other leads a solitary life. A Back Bay waterman, Romy Waterfield, worked with a Johns Hopkins scientist who thought he had verified two instances in which whistling swans, having lost mates, had remated. "I'd say that was debatable," said Waterfield, unshaken.